RICHMOND

ESSENTIAL

English

PRE-INTERMEDIATE
Coursebook with CD-ROM

COURSE

3

GREAT! WHAT ABOUT YOU? YES, OF COURSE
I LOVE IT THAT'S A GREAT IDEA
HAVE A GOOD TRIP
HAVE A GOOD HOLIDAY
OH, REALLY? IT'S THE SAME IN MY LANGUAGE
YES, YOU'RE RIGHT
NICE TO MEET YOU, TOO
HERE YOU ARE
SEE YOU LATER
HURRY UP! EXCUSE ME, PLEASE!
LET'S GO

Main author:
PAUL SELIGSON

Richmond
PUBLISHING

www.richmondelt.com/essentialenglish

Contents

2

3

What was the weather like?

Speaking

1 You have two minutes to learn all you can about your partner. Then tell the class three interesting things you remember.

Is this your first lesson at this school?

Where exactly are you from?

2 (1.1) What's the weather like in your country in different seasons? What's your favourite type of weather? Word Bank 1, p. 64.

In summer, it's quite warm and sometimes very hot! The rest of the year it's very cold.

Grammar

3 (1.2) Listen to part of a conversation between Jill and Sam and complete the Grammar box. Why wasn't the hot weather a problem for Sam?

be like

Jill:	What _____ the weather like in Egypt?
Sam:	_____ _____ _____ . But it didn't matter.
Jill:	What _____ the people _____ ?
Sam:	They _____ _____ . Really _____ .

Use *be like* to describe somebody or something.

AB, p. 79. Ex. 2 ▶

Listening

4 (1.3) Listen to the complete conversation and order questions 1–7 correctly. Then listen again and answer the questions.

1 Why didn't Sam tell Jill before? ☐
2 Did he stay in a hotel? ☐
3 Was the hotel expensive? ☐
4 Why didn't they visit Cairo? ☐
5 What was the diving like? ☐
6 Didn't he want to see the Pyramids? ☐
7 Who did Sam go with? *1*

Grammar

5 Match the question types in the Grammar box to the question types 1–7 in Exercise 4.

6 Complete the Grammar box with these letters:

A = auxiliary verb
B = verb *be*
I = infinitive verb
N = negative auxiliary
S = subject
Q = question

AB, p. 79. Ex. 3 ▶

Q	Word order in questions				
3	Yes / No *be* questions:	1 _B_	2 _S_		
_	Other Yes / No questions:	1 __	2 __	3 __	
_	*Wh-?* *be* questions:	1 __	2 __	3 __	
_	Other *Wh-?* questions:	1 __	2 __	3 __	4 __
_	Negative Yes / No questions:	1 __	2 __	3 __	
_ _	Negative *Wh-?* questions:	1 __	2 __	3 __	4 __

Is word order in questions similar in your language?

Listening

7 Read the headlines and look at the photos. What do you think happened?

Himalayan rescue team comes back empty-handed

Brave Californians save homes from forest fire!

8 (1.4) Listen to news 1 and 2. Write T (true) or F (false).

1 The weather's awful now near Mount Everest. ___

2 The weather was awful all day yesterday. ___

3 The rescue team thought they found the tour group. ___

4 The fire started three days ago in Arizona. ___

5 The police asked people to leave but they refused. ___

6 Hundreds of people helped firefighters all day and all night. ___

Pronunciation

9 (1.5) One verb in 1–3 has an 'extra' syllable in the past. Which one? Listen and check.

1	helped	moved	started
2	disappeared	ended	worked
3	stopped	tried	wanted

10 Are the vowel sounds in these irregular verbs the (S) same or (D) different? What are the infinitive forms?

1	went	left	_S_
2	had	made	___
3	was	got	___
4	grew	said	___
5	found	thought	___
6	told	took	___

11 In pairs, list ten irregular verbs you know. Word Bank 13, p.76.

Speaking

12 In pairs, ask and answer about a holiday with memorable weather. Each ✳ = one missing word. Try to ask more questions. Remember your partner's story to tell the class.

Where exactly ✳ ✳ go?

Who ✳ ✳ ✳ with?

How ✳ ✳ ✳ get there?

How long ✳ ✳ stay?

What ✳ ✳ weather like?

✳ didn't ✳ stay longer?

What exactly ✳ you do?

✳ didn't ✳ like about it?

✳ ✳ like ✳ go there again?

1B Saving the planet

Reading

1 Study the poster for 20 seconds. Then answer in pairs.

  1 What can you see in the poster?

  2 Do you know this film? What do you think it's about?

  3 What do you know about Al Gore?

2 Read the TV trailer to check your answers. Then circle the correct options, 1–4, below.

By far the most terrifying film you will ever see.

an inconvenient truth
A GLOBAL WARNING

> On Tuesday evening Channel 4 is showing *An Inconvenient Truth*. This Academy Award-winning documentary film is about climate change and global warming. Presented by former US Vice President Al Gore, it shows exactly how we are destroying the planet. For example, every day our factory chimneys and cars pollute the air, planes use enormous amounts of petrol and our roads and buildings eat up more and more of the natural world. He explains how the climate is changing and gives scary examples of how the world is getting warmer.
>
> This was and still is a very powerful film and it helped Al Gore to win the Nobel Peace Prize. But do people fully understand the dangers, even today? Are we actually changing the way we live? Does everybody believe climate change is really happening? After the film Channel 4 is holding a discussion between two scientific experts with very different opinions. Don't miss it!

1 Our climate's changing *naturally / because of global warming*.

2 The text includes the name of *one prize / two prizes*.

3 After the film, there's a discussion between two experts who *agree / disagree*.

4 Does the title of the film mean we don't **A** really want to know about climate change?

                                               B believe what scientists tell us about climate change?

Pronunciation

3 (1.6) Put the words in the correct stress group. Use the pink words in the text to help you. Listen and check.

1 ● ●	2 ● ●
climate	*repeat*

~~climate~~ danger destroy former
global planet pollute ~~repeat~~

4 Complete the rules with *nouns*, *adjectives* or *verbs*.

Rules

Most two-syllable _____ and _____ have the stress on the first syllable.

Most two-syllable _____ have the stress on the second syllable.

Speaking

5 In pairs, ask and answer the questions. Which of you is a green traveller?

Are you a green traveller or a 'private polluter'?

How often do you …?

1 ride a bike

2 travel by plane

3 get a train

4 go on a ferry

5 walk to work / university

6 get a bus

7 use the underground

8 travel by tram

Not very often. Maybe twice a week.

Grammar

6 Match sentences 1–3 to rules A–C.

Present simple and Present continuous

1 The world's climate is changing.
2 I fly on business once a month.
3 Do people fully understand the dangers?

A Use the Present simple for regular actions.
B Some verbs aren't normally used in the continuous form.
C Use the Present continuous for actions happening now.

AB, p. 80. Ex. 3 ▶

Tip
Seven verbs not usually used in the continuous form are *think, have, know, understand, see, hear* and *believe*.

7 Complete the sentences with the correct form of the verbs.

1 I _____ a small car. It _____ much petrol. *(have, not use)*

2 I _____ a plastic bag now but we usually only _____ paper ones. *(carry, buy)*

3 Today my wife _____ a dress from Oxfam. She _____ new clothes any more – except shoes and underwear. *(wear, not buy)*

4 Our grandchildren always _____ the bus to school and _____ home. I never _____ them in the car but today my wife _____ them because they _____ to a party. *(take, walk, drive, collect, go)*

5 _____ you _____ most people today recycle plastic, glass, paper and metal? *(think?)*

Listening

8 (1.7) Listen to Si and Bess. Then circle the correct answers to the questions.

Environment Day
𝄞 June at Brown's College
Come and learn about these important issues:
pollution   recycling
            climate change
global warming

1 Who's organising the 'Environment Day'?
Bess / Si / Mark

2 They're having the 'Environment Day' on *4th / 5th / 14th* June.

3 The lecture on climate change is happening *at 8.30 / in the morning / after lunch.*

4 Si wants Bess to *talk at the meeting / pick somebody up / organise lunch.*

Grammar

9 Study the yellow verbs from the phone message. Choose the correct answers.

We're having a special 'Environment Day'. Mark Barnard is giving a lecture. He's arriving at 8.30. I'm meeting the other speakers at 8.15. We're having lunch at 12.30.

A The verbs are in the *Present continuous / Present simple.*
B Si's talking about a *past / present / future* time.
C The actions are *plans / regular activities / possibilities.*

10 ⬜ Get cards from your teacher. Ask and answer questions to complete the arrangements for the 'Environment day'.

A: *What's happening at 10.30?*   B: *The students are having a break.*

Speaking

11 In small groups, ask and answer about your plans or arrangements for tomorrow. Note two or three interesting answers to tell the class.

Mario 1.30.   Lunch Jazz café Lucia.

Mario's having lunch at the Jazz Café at 1.30 with Lucia!

I'm going to relax by the pool

Speaking

1 In pairs, ask and answer the questions.

1 When was the last time you stayed in a hotel?

2 What's important for people when they're choosing a hotel?

3 Decide on three facilities you always look for in a hotel.

2 Did you say these facilities? Match the words to the facilities. What are the other facilities, 1–12? Now choose the three that are most important for you and say why.

☐ air-conditioning / heating   ☐ cable TV   ☐ Internet access   ☐ laundry

6 mini bar   ☐ room service   11 spa and sauna

1	**2** PPV	**3**	**4**
5	**6**	**7**	**8**
9	**10**	**11**	**12** €

Reading

3 Read the hotel brochure. Write (T) true or (F) false. Which country do you think this hotel is in?

1 You get a bus from the airport to the hotel. ___

2 You can get drinks next to the swimming pool. ___

3 You can go fishing alone. ___

4 The night club is open all night. ___

5 There are snakes near the hotel. ___

6 It has an expensive restaurant. ___

4 (1.8) What does get mean in sentences 1 and 2 above? Word Bank 2, p. 65.

Listening

5 (1.9) Listen to Dave and Mona.

1 Is Dave going to stay at the hotel for work or pleasure?

2 What is the relationship between Dave and Mona?

6 Listen again and tick the facilities he's going to use on the hotel brochure.

The Smiling Alligator Hotel

☐ *transfer from airport by Land Rover*

☐ *swimming pool, sauna and gym*

☐ *wonderful restaurant with wide range of seafood dishes*

☐ *all food and non-alcoholic drinks included in the price!*

☐ *boats for fishing trips – with or without guide (from 9am daily)*

☐ *tropical rainforest, ideal for picnics or a nice walk (no dangerous animals!)*

☐ *night club and casino (open 10pm–4am)*

Tip

Remember we write *going to* but we usually say 'gonna'.

Reading

7 (1.10) Dave's in 'The Smiling Alligator' restaurant. Read the dialogues and choose the answers to questions 1 to 4. Listen, check and repeat. In pairs, practise the dialogues.

1 Are you ready to order?

  A Can I have another minute, please?

  B No. Go away.

  C I'm fine, thanks. And you?

2 I'll have the soup for starters and then the steak.

  A And for the main course?

  B What would you like for starters?

  C All right, sir. Rare, medium, well-done?

3 How about dessert?

  A I'd like the salad.

  B I won't have anything, thanks.

  C I think I'll have the chicken.

4 Can I have the bill?

  A Certainly, sir. I'll get it for you now.

  B Do you have a credit card?

  C Thank you, sir.

Grammar

8 Study the yellow examples in Exercises 5, 6 and 7. Then complete the rules with *will*, *won't* or *be going to*.

will / won't and **be going to**

1 I _____ have the soup for starters.

2 I _____ have anything, thanks.

3 I _____ spend the first day by the pool.

Use _____ for decisions we make as we're talking, without planning.

Use _____ for when we plan a future action in advance of doing it.

AB, p. 81. Ex. 5 ▶

9 (1.11) Dave meets a woman, Camila, at the hotel. Match A–E to 1–5. Listen and check. Be careful with *I'll*. Then repeat the answers.

Dave

A It's nearly lunchtime.

B Are you ready?

C What would you like to drink?

D I haven't got any money with me.

E Would you like to come for a walk?

Camila

1 Nearly. I'll meet you outside.

2 That's OK. I'll pay.

3 I'll have a quick swim and then we can go and eat.

4 No thanks. I'll stay here and sunbathe.

5 I'll have a glass of orange juice.

Speaking

10 In pairs, imagine you're at the hotel.

A: Make some suggestions and invitations.
B: Make a decision. Swap roles.

A: *Would you like to come for a walk?*

B: *No, I think I'll stay here and read my book.*

11 In threes, compare plans for the next few days. Find three things you all have in common.

A: *I'm going to buy some winter clothes on Saturday.*

B: *Me too.*

C: *I'm not. I think I'll go to bed early tonight. I'm really tired.*

A very bad journey

Speaking

1  **(1.12)** Name four problems you can have when you're travelling. Word Bank 3, p. 66.

Listening

2 **(1.13)** Listen to a radio show about awful journeys. Are cartoons 1–8 in the right order?

3 Which six problems from Word Bank 3, p. 66 does the caller, Phil, talk about? Listen again and check.

4 In pairs, answer questions 1–6. Then listen again and shadow read the audioscript on page 107 to check. Follow the text and pause briefly each time you see /.

1 Where was he going for a meeting?

2 Why did he decide to go by train?

3 Why did it take a long time to get to the station?

4 What four things were the people at the station doing?

5 What was the journey on the train like and why?

6 How was he feeling when he finally got to the meeting?

Grammar

5 Complete these sentences in the Grammar box with the verbs. Choose the correct rule.

feel go pour sit stand wake up

Past continuous

When I _____ , it _____ with rain.

Some _____ , others _____ on their bags.

I _____ very well.

Where _____ you _____ ?

Which are finished actions? Which are unfinished?

Use the Past continuous for actions that were *happening / finished* at a time in the past.

AB, p. 82. Ex. 3 ▶

Pronunciation

6 (1.14) Listen to how the speaker pronounces *was* and *were*. Practise saying the examples in the same way.

Speaking

7 In pairs, remember the story from the pictures in Exercise 2.
A: Tell pictures 1, 3, 5 and 7.
B: Tell pictures 2, 4, 6 and 8.
Then swap roles.

A: *When Phil woke up, it was …*

8 In threes, invent a bad journey. Choose some problems from Word Bank 3, p. 66. Use the Past simple and Past continuous. Make notes using the table below.

When / happen?	
Where / going?	
Who / with?	
What / happen?	
What went wrong?	

9 Tell the class your story. Who had a *really, really* bad journey?

Yesterday we were driving to the beach. It was really sunny and we were feeling great. There were lots of cars, because everyone was going on holiday. Then our car stopped! We ran out of petrol and …

Should I or shouldn't I?

Speaking

1 Complete the questionnaire. In pairs, compare your answers. Are they similar?

Do we give kids too much freedom?

1 How did you get to school when you were a kid?

2 How old were you when you first went to school alone or without an adult?

3 How old were you when you first travelled a long distance alone?

4 Did your parents give you a lot of freedom when you were younger?

5 Do you think kids today have a lot of freedom?

Reading

2 (1.15) Look at the photos. Where do the people live? What can you see? Word Bank 3, p. 66.

3 Read the article. Write T (true) or F (false).

1 Lenore lost her son in New York. ___

2 Izzy didn't want to make the journey alone. ___

3 Izzy had some money. ___

4 Lenore lives a mile from the store. ___

5 People are interested in the story. ___

6 Everyone thinks we should let children travel alone. ___

Listening

4 (1.16) Leonore's talking to Izzy. Listen and guess what's she's going to say next, 1–6. Use *because*. Then listen and check.

1 You shouldn't play in the yard because _____ .

4 You should eat green _____ .

2 You should go to bed early because tomorrow you have _____ .

5 You shouldn't watch violent _____ .

3 You shouldn't eat _____ .

6 You shouldn't climb _____ .

Going Home Alone!

Lenore Skenazy, a Manhattan mother, left her son, Izzy, in a large store in New York. She gave him a subway map, a bus ticket and a dollar but she didn't give him a cell phone. Izzy had to get home from the store on his own. It was two miles through downtown New York. He did the journey successfully. He took the bus, the subway, asked for directions and arrived home very happy. That's not very difficult, right? But Izzy was only nine years old. Why did his mother let him do this?

Because, she says, Izzy wanted an adventure. Now, the story is big news and people are asking a lot of questions. Was she right to let her son travel on the subway alone? Should we give children freedom like this? Is it safe? Is Lenore a bad mother? Some think it's a good idea. They say we should let our children be independent. We shouldn't protect them all the time. What do you think? We'd love to hear your opinions. E-mail us at viewsonthenews.com.

Grammar

Study the yellow examples and circle the right rules.

should / shouldn't

We _____ protect children all the time.

Children _____ eat green vegetables.

_____ we give children freedom?

Should has *the same / a different* form for all persons.
To make a question use *Do you should…? / Should you…?*
Use / Don't use to + verb after *should*.
Use *should* to say something is a *good / bad* idea.

AB, p. 83. Ex. 3 ▶

5 What's your opinion? Complete these sentences with *should* or *shouldn't*.

1 Parents _____ let young children play together without an adult.

2 Children _____ have a TV and computer in their rooms.

3 Kids _____ choose what time to go to bed.

4 Children _____ always obey their parents.

5 Parents _____ let kids eat fast food.

6 Parents _____ help children with their homework

6 In pairs, compare answers and give a reason for your opinion. Use these phrases.

Agreeing and disagreeing.

I completely agree with you.

Yes, you're right.

I feel the same.

I partly agree because … .

I have a different opinion.

I don't agree with you at all!

A: *We should let children play together without an adult.*

B: *I completely agree with you. They can't play freely with an adult there.*

Speaking

7 In pairs, decide what these people should do? Compare answers with another pair. Do you all agree?

Location vacation!

Speaking

1 (1.17) Where do you usually go on holiday? What are your three favourite holiday activities?
Word Bank 4, p. 67.

Listening

2 (1.18) Listen to Ana and Bob talking about their holidays. Where does Ana get her ideas from?

> films   friends   the Internet   magazines or papers
> travel agents   TV programmes

3 (1.19) Listen to the rest of their conversation. Where does Bob get his ideas from?

4 Listen again and circle the correct option.

1 Ana's friends tell her where
  a to go.   b not to go.   c to go and not to go.

2 For his holiday last year, Bob went
  a alone.   b by train.   c to Scotland.

3 Going on *Location Vacations* is getting
  a expensive.   b popular.   c difficult.

4 On the holiday tour, Bob went to see
  a some friends. b lots of places. c a new film.

5 Where's Bob's next holiday going to be?
  a the USA.   b the Caribbean   c not sure

Reading

5 Work in groups of four. In 45 seconds, read about one 'Location Vacation' each and then tell your group what you remember about it.

The nominations for the Top Location Vacation of the last five years are …

Pan's Labyrinth

Visit (1) the beautiful hills near (2) the city of Segovia and see where (3) the magical fantasy film *Pan's Labyrinth* was made. Director Guillermo del Toro chose this area for his film because of its beauty and soon (4) the whole area is going to become (5) a national park. You can go on (6) a walking holiday over the hills and stay at local bed and breakfasts. And of course, you have to visit (7) the historical city of Segovia with its wonderful churches and old medieval streets.

Darjeeling Limited

Darjeeling Limited didn't win an Oscar but its locations are a traveller's dream! The film is based on a real train journey and you can take the trip yourself on the very expensive and luxurious 'Palace on Wheels'. This travels through colourful Rajasthan, stopping often so that travellers can visit palaces and other beautiful places. For a trip that is not so expensive you should take the Darjeeling–Himalayan Railway. It goes through the famous tea country. You travel in original 1890s train carriages – it's an amazing holiday.

Atonement

To make the popular film *Atonement* the director went to a beautiful part of the English countryside – Shropshire. The wonderful house in the film is Stokesay Court and now you can go on special tours of the house. The tour lasts an hour and shows you the different rooms and outdoor locations that are in the film. At the end of the tour you get a real English tea! Near the House are many small, country pubs you can visit. A favourite place for the actors in the film, including Keira Knightley, was The Feathers at Ludlow!

The Bourne Ultimatum

Do you like railway stations? Well, *The Bourne Ultimatum* has an important scene at Waterloo Station in London and lots of Location Vacation people go there for a visit! But if you really want to follow Bourne's adventures you should take the ferry from Tarifa in Spain to Tangier in Morocco to see where the big chases were filmed. Berlin is also important in this film series and when you are in Germany you should also visit the spy museum in Leipzig! It's incredible.

6 Which holiday is good for somebody who likes … ?

1 being outside?

2 journeys?

3 old buildings?

4 doing exercise?

5 good views?

Grammar

7 Match the yellow examples 1–7, to rules, 1–3.

> **Articles**
>
> 1 Use *the* when you know which one. _____
> 2 Use *the* for something there is only one of. 2, 3
> 3 Use *a / an* when you don't know which one. _____

8 Find other examples in the texts where articles are NOT used because it's

1 the name of a town.

2 the name of a country.

3 the name of a film.

4 a plural noun used generally.

5 the name of a station.

AB, p. 84. Ex. 1 ▶

Speaking

9 Make questions for a holiday survey.

> 1 Where ✳ ✳ usually go ✳ holiday?
>
> 2 What ✳ ✳ usually do?
>
> 3 Who ✳ ✳ usually go with?
>
> 4 Where ✳ ✳ going next year?
>
> 5 What would ✳ like ✳ do there?
>
> 6 Where ✳ ✳ go last year?
>
> 7 What ✳ ✳ last holiday like?
>
> 8 What exactly ✳ ✳ do?

10 In pairs, ask and answer the questions. Remember any coincidences to tell the class.

We both usually go to Turkey …

Go to **Phrasebook 1** p. 77 ▶   Go to **Essential Grammar 1** p. 112 ▶

Revision

1A **1** (1.20) Correct ten more mistakes with verb forms. Listen and check.

Rita: So, Alan, ~~you are~~ *are you* really coming over here to Germany?

Alan: Yes! Next month. February.

Rita: Cool. Where do you staying?

Alan: I'm in Bonn. Is that quite close to Cologne not?

Rita: That's right. They're right next to each other. How long you staying over here?

Alan: Two weeks. Seven days for work and then seven days for fun.

Rita: Great! Well, coming and visit me in Cologne. Do you like to stay in my apartment? I have a spare room.

Alan: Yeah. If it not going to be a problem ...

Rita: No! I'd love to have you here. We have a really good time. We can visit the museums and galleries ...

Alan: Don't there quite a lot of nightclubs in Cologne too?

Rita: Hundreds. We can to go clubbing if you like.

Alan: Yeah! Definitely. Hey, by the way, what the weather will be like? Will it be cold?

Rita: Probably, but sometimes is quite sunny here in February.

1B **2** Circle the correct option.

1 It's the last day of our holiday, so *we buy / we're buying* some souvenirs to take home.

2 Julia isn't at home. I think *she swimming / she's swimming* on the beach.

3 My grandparents *usually go / are usually going* on holiday in May.

4 *Do you get / Are you getting* the bus to the party?

5 *I don't believe / I'm not believing* that story!

6 Keep quiet! The baby *sleeps / is sleeping*.

7 The instructions for this TV are really long. *Do you understand / Are you understanding?*

8 Stavros *doesn't play / isn't playing* football today because he doesn't feel well.

3 Play WHAT AM I DOING? Get cards from your teacher. A: Mime an action. B & C: Guess what A is doing in 30 seconds.

1C **4** Complete with *will* or *going to* and the verbs.

Nick: Right, let's have lunch. The menu looks great. Steak, lamb...

José: I think I (1) *'ll have* (have) a salad to start.

Nick: A salad? That's not like you.

José: I don't want a big lunch because I (2) _____ (go) to the gym this afternoon.

Nick: The gym? You?

José: Yes! Judy wants to do the same. She (3) _____ (come) to the gym this afternoon too. And we (4) _____ (not / get) the bus to work anymore. We (5) _____ (cycle) there every day.

Nick: What a great idea!

José: Oh, that reminds me. I need to speak to Judy about this afternoon. I (6) _____ (call) her now.

Nick: OK. I think I (7) _____ (choose) something to drink.

5 In pairs, ask and answer about weekend plans. Find out as much as you can in three minutes.

A: *What are you going to do on Saturday?*

B: *I'm going to a party in the evening.*

1D **6** (1.21) Listen and complete Brad's story.

1 The story happened on ___Friday___ night.

2 Brad and his girlfriend saw a man who was sitting in _____.

3 The man was about _____ years old.

4 The man had blood on his _____.

5 The man said he was buying some _____ for his grandchildren.

6 Brad called an ambulance on his _____.

7 How many irregular verbs can you remember? Word Bank 13, p. 76.

Song: *Singing in the rain* by Gene Kelly

To find the words, google lyric + the name of the song.

To find the video, google video + the name of the song and singer.

8 Look at the photos. Write what the people were doing yesterday.

1 *He was reading a book.*
2 _____
3 _____
4 _____

1E 9 In threes, play WHAT SHOULD I DO? Get cards from your teacher.

10 Read the email. In pairs, give answers using *should / shouldn't* for 1–3.

Hi!

How are you? Can I ask for some help? I'm coming to your country next month. It's my first time there and I need some advice. I don't want to be a boring tourist – please tell me what I should do! **(1) What do people in your country eat?** **(2) Where do they go in the evenings? (3) What cities or places should I visit?**

Thanks,
Eva

1F 11 Complete with *a*, *an*, *the* or nothing.

Mamma Mia!

Take Oscar winner Meryl Streep, ex-James Bond Pierce Brosnan, (1)_____ first-time director and (2)_____ songs of Abba and what do you have? The hit movie of 2008: *Mamma Mia!*

(3)_____ film is set on (4)_____ Greek island, named Kalokairi. But (5)_____ fans of the movie who want to go on (6)_____ location vacation can still visit all (7)_____ beaches. They were actually filmed on (8)_____ Skopelos, an island off (9)_____ East coast of (10)_____ Greece. (11)_____ tourists rarely visit the island so it is a traditional place. In fact, it is still (12)_____ agricultural country and well-known for producing (13)_____ fruit and nuts. Skopelos is also famous for (14)_____ major archaeological discovery. In 1936, (15)_____ team of archaeologists discovered gold objects and (16)_____ sword from Ancient Greece. So with movie connections, good food, and (17)_____ presence of the Ancient Greeks, Skopelos is (18)_____ ideal spot for anyone's location vacation!

Which film is better?

Speaking

1 Complete the questionnaire. In pairs, compare answers. Any big differences?

Are you into **movies**?

1 In an average week, how many hours of TV do you watch?

Less than 6 hours ☐ More than 6 but less than 15 ☐ More than 15 hours ☐

2 Which of these do you watch regularly?

comedies ☐ documentaries ☐ movies ☐ news ☐ reality TV ☐ soaps ☐

others? ☐ (which?) _____

3 Which of these do you prefer and how often do you … ?

watch films on TV
once or twice a week ☐ 3 or 4 times a week ☐ less often ☐

rent a movie
once or twice a month ☐ once or twice a week ☐ less often ☐

go the cinema
once or twice a year ☐ once or twice a month ☐ more often ☐

4 Do you have any favourite actors, directors or genres of film? Which one(s)?

5 What was the last film you saw? What was it like?

6 What's the next film you're planning to see? Why?

2 (2.1) What do you know about the films in the posters? Think of three adjectives to describe the Batman films. Word Bank 5, p.68.

WELCOME TO A WORLD WITHOUT RULES.

CHRISTIAN BALE   MICHAEL CAINE   LIAM NEESON   KATIE HOLMES   GARY OLDMAN   and MORGAN FREEMAN

BATMAN BEGINS

CHRISTIAN BALE   MICHAEL CAINE   HEATH LEDGER   GARY OLDMAN   AARON ECKHART   MAGGIE GYLLENHAAL   and MORGAN FREEMAN

A film by CHRISTOPHER NOLAN

THE DARK KNIGHT

JULY 18   WWW.THEDARKKNIGHT.COM

Listening

3 (2.2) Jo and Lee went to a 'Batman Evening'. Listen and answer.

1 Where are they now?

2 Which did they prefer: *Batman Begins* or *The Dark Knight*?

4 Listen again and order the names, 1–7. There's one extra one. What else did you understand this time?

Batman Begins ☐
The Dark Knight ☐
Christian Bale ☐
Heath Ledger ☐
Jack Nicholson ☐
Katie Holmes ☐
The Joker ☐

5 Complete the dialogue. Listen again to check.

Jo: Phew – That was a (1)_____ film!

Lee: Yeah, about two and a half hours! (2)_____ longer than *Batman Begins*.

Jo: But I really (3)_____ it. Pass the sugar.

Lee: Me (4)_____. It's darker, (5)_____ serious and definitely more violent than *Batman Begins*.

Jo: And Heath Ledger was (6)_____ as The Joker. Much scarier than Jack Nicholson, though Nicholson was a bigger (7)_____.

Lee: Yes, Ledger was a (8)_____ actor. Pity he died before they finished (9)_____ it.

Jo: Yeah. Maggie what's her (10)_____ – you know, the actress who plays Batman's ex (11)_____ is very good too. Lovely.

Lee: Yeah, she's more interesting (12)_____ Katie Holmes was in *Batman Begins*.

Jo: So, do you (13)_____ *The Dark Knight* is better or worse than *Batman Begins*?

Lee: Better. Much better. (14)_____. I like them both but *The Dark Knight* is (15)_____. It's more powerful.

Jo: I (16)_____, and more intelligent too. And this has to be the best (17)_____ in town.

Grammar

6 Study the rules and yellow words in Exercise 5. Match each example to a rule, A–E.

> **Rules**
>
> **To form a comparative adjective**
>
> **A** One-syllable adjectives + -*er*.
>
> **B** One-syllable adjectives ending in a vowel and a consonant, double the final consonant + -*er*.
>
> **C** Two-syllable adjectives ending in -*y* + -*ier*.
>
> **D** *more* + adjective for most adjectives with two or more syllables.
>
> **E** Two important irregular adjectives: *good / better* *bad / worse*

(AB, p. 86. Ex. 5 ▶)

Pronunciation

7 (2.3) Listen to five sentences comparing Katie Holmes and Maggie Gyllenhaal. Write down the comparative adjectives. How is *than* pronounced?

Speaking

8 In pairs, compare the actors with these adjectives.

> attractive   good (actor)   dark (hair)   rich
> short (hair)   successful   tall   young

Denzel's younger than Jack.

Penelope's got longer hair than Reece.

9 In pairs, compare two films you both know. Use adjectives from Word Bank 5, p. 68. Which is funnier or more interesting? Which film is the class's favourite?

Have you read *Duma Key*?

Listening

1 **(2.4)** Listen and match the three texts to the types in the box. Which are your three favourite types of text? Where and when do you usually read them?

> (auto)biographies   brochures   comics   easy readers   magazines
> newspapers   novels   poems   puzzles   screenplays   subtitles   webpages

Reading

2 Do you know anything about the men on the book covers? Compare what the men look like.

> *They're both wearing glasses.*

3 In pairs, complete the chart. A: do Ishiguro. B: do King. Then swap answers.

	Kasuo Ishiguro	Stephen King
Age		
Nationality		
Books		
Education		
Family		
Prizes		
Current activities		

Kazuo Ishiguro was born in Nagasaki, Japan, on November 8, 1954. When he was five he moved to Britain with his family and they never went back to Japan. Ishiguro studied English and Philosophy at university and wrote his first book, *A Pale View of Hills*, in 1982. It was a great success. Since then he has written five novels and seven screenplays and has won several prizes. He wrote his third and most famous novel, *The Remains of the Day*, in 1989 and won the Booker prize in the same year. It then became a film in 1993, starring Emma Thompson and Anthony Hopkins. Ishiguru is internationally famous and literary critics all over the world have praised his work. His books can now be read in over 30 languages. 'Ish', as he is known to his friends, lives in London with his wife, Lorna, and daughter, Naomi. He spends his time writing, giving interviews and going on long book tours.

Stephen King was born in Portland, Maine on September 21st, 1947. He studied English at Maine University where he met his wife, Tabitha. They married in 1971 and King wrote his first book, Carrie, in 1973. He has written over 200 stories and has sold over 350 million books, making him America's best-selling author. King writes thrillers and adventure stories but is really famous for his horror stories. Many have become films, including *The Shining* and *Misery*. He also published a book on the Internet in 2000 but this wasn't successful. In 1999 King had a bad car accident. Since then, his health has been poor and he hasn't published a lot. Although many critics haven't liked his work, he received a major prize in 2003 and his last book, *Duma Key* was a bestseller. Today he and Tabitha, a novelist too, have three kids, Naomi, Joseph and Owen and still live in Maine. King also writes about pop for Rolling Stone magazine and loves going to Boston Red Sox games.

4 In pairs, answer the questions. Write I (Ishiguru) or K (King) or B (both).

   1 Who lives in the same area where he was born? ___

   2 Who started writing first? ___

   3 Who's won more than one literary prize? ___

   4 Whose daughter is called Naomi? ___

   5 Who hasn't been well recently? ___

   6 Whose books are also films? ___

   7 Who has published online? ___

> **Tip**
>
> *who's* = is or has   *whose* = possessive
> *who's* and *whose* are pronounced /huːz/.

5 (2.5) Can you remember what happened in these years? Read and listen to the biographies to check.

1947	1954	1982	1989
1993	1999	2000	2003

Grammar

6 Study the text. Complete the Grammar box with *have*, *has* or *hasn't*.

> **Present perfect**
>
> ➕ Ishiguru _____ published books and screenplays.
> ➖ King _____ written many books recently.
> ❓ _____ you read any of their books?
> ✔✘ Yes, I _____ . / No, I haven't.
>
> **Form** the Present perfect with _____ or _____ + **past participle**.
> **Use** it to talk about something that happened before now without giving the time or date.
> *King* **has written** *over 200 stories.*

AB, p. 87. Ex. 4 ▶

7 Look at the yellow past participles in the text. Is the Past simple of these verbs the same or different? Check with a partner.

8 Test your partner on past participles. Go to Word Bank 13, p. 76.

9 (2.6) Listen and complete the dialogue. Practise it in pairs.

   A: _____ the new James Bond film?

   B: No, I _____ . Is it any good?

   A: Yes, it's brilliant. I saw it last month.

   B: _____ *Casino Royale*? That's my favourite.

   A: Yes, _____ . But I _____ the new one _____ .

Speaking

10 Write down the name of a recent film, a TV programme and a book. In pairs, ask and answer questions about them. Do you have similar tastes?

   A: Have you seen the film *Transformers 2*?

   B: No, I haven't. Is it good?

   A: No, it's terrible!

11 In pairs, write a questionnaire. Use three of these ideas and add two more. Survey the class then tell them your results.

> **How many ... ?**
>
> clothes / buy this week
> countries / visit
> different places / live in
> exams / take
> books in English / read
> films / see
> text messages / send this week
> hours / spend 'googling' this week
> vehicles / own

How many countries have you been to?

Apart from my own, only two others ...

A spider for breakfast?

Speaking

1 (2.7) Think of three adjectives to describe your personality. Word Bank 5, p.68.

2 In pairs, answer the questions in this TV magazine survey.

Reality shows – are they here to stay?

1 Have you seen Big Brother? Are you a reality show fan?

2 Why are reality shows so popular?

3 Do you think people will get tired of them soon?

4 What sort of people go on reality shows?

Reading

3 Read the first two paragraphs of the TV magazine article quickly. Which picture is the location of the new show? What do you think the rest of the text will be about?

Do you want to be on tv?

Reality TV shows are everywhere these days. Everybody seems to love watching them and helping to decide who's going to win or lose. But how about actually taking part in a show yourself? Well, now you can! Producers are looking for contestants for a new reality show starting in three months' time. Perhaps one of them is you?

It has an exciting location. No, not on an island and it's not your normal Big Brother type house either! That isn't exciting enough for this show! It's going to be in Romania – remember Dracula? – in a castle just like his, in the middle of a big, dark forest! Contestants have to find their own food in the forest and if there isn't enough, they have to eat bats and spiders! Still interested? Read on! …

4 Read the rest of the article to check if you were right. In pairs, find adjectives to describe the people, 1–4.

1 'She likes everyone!'

2 'She sometimes gets angry!'

3 'He tells good jokes!'

4 'He doesn't like talking to people.'

What are the producers looking for? Well, a good mix of people – friendly, serious, funny – even a little aggressive (but not TOO aggressive!) The most important thing is a strong personality. Contestants can't be too shy or too quiet. Good contestants are often extroverts and very energetic. And of course, age is important too. If you're under 18, then, sorry, you're too young. Try again when you're older! But older readers, please don't think you're not young enough to be on the show! Remember Peter Fields last year – he was eighty five!!

If you think you're right for the show, email your details now, telling us why! Who knows? Perhaps we will all vote for (or against!) you!

Grammar

5 Study the yellow words in the text. Complete the Grammar box with *too* or *enough*.

> **too and enough**
>
> If you're over 18, you're old _____ for the show.
> If you're under 18, you're _____ young.
> So, if you're only 17, you aren't old _____ .
>
> Use _____ + **adjective** if it's 'more than necessary' and negative.
> Use *not + be + **adjective** + _____ if it's 'not the necessary level' and negative.

AB, p. 88. Ex. 2 ▶

Listening

6 (2.8) Listen to the producers talking about three applicants. Circle the correct answers. Who do they choose?

 **Brad**
 **Laura**
 **Angie**

1 Brad's *intelligent / energetic*.

2 Brad likes *going to the cinema / reading*.

3 Brad's *interesting / boring*.

4 Laura does *sports / art*.

5 Laura never gets *violent / angry*.

6 Angie's *45 / 55*.

7 Angie has *strong / no* opinions.

8 Angie has *unusual / boring* hobbies.

Pronunciation

7 (2.9) In pairs, complete the phrases with the words. Some of the first letters are given to help you. Listen and check. Stress the underlined words and the gapped words.

> bit boring certainly else energetic intelligent
> interesting out really suppose sure win

1 He's not <u>bad</u> I s_____.

2 He's <u>quite</u> i_____.

3 But is he e_____ enough?

4 A bit b_____?

5 Who _____ is <u>there</u>?

6 She's _____ energetic.

7 I <u>think</u> she's a b_____ too <u>calm</u>.

8 <u>That's</u> no <u>good</u>. So <u>Laura's</u> _____.

9 She's _____ not too <u>shy</u>.

10 I'm not _____.

11 I <u>don't</u> think she's i_____ enough.

12 <u>OK</u>. You _____. We'll <u>have</u> her.

Speaking

8 In groups of three, get cards from your teacher. Roleplay choosing a contestant for the show. Do you agree with the rest of the class?

A: *So, who have we got?*
B: *Well, I really like Brad. He's gorgeous!*

Do you love your computer?

Speaking

1 (2.10) Name three nouns and three verbs connected with computers. Word Bank 6, p. 69.

2 Complete this survey. In pairs, compare answers. Any big differences?

> **Are you a computer geek?**
>
> Is your computer the most important thing in your life? Take part in our survey to find out how important computers are to people today!
>
> ❶ How many computers do you have at home / work?
> ❷ Do you have any other devices to go online?
> ❸ How often do you use them and what for?
> ❹ How long can you spend without using e-mail, msn, facebook or google?
> ❺ How do you feel and what do you do when they go wrong?

Reading

3 In pairs, describe the cartoons. What are they thinking?

4 Read the article and match each cartoon to the type of user it represents.

What kind of computer user are you?

☐ **Computer geeks** are _____ most passionate about technology and spend all their free time at their computer. They often use 'geek speak' (special computer vocabulary) and it's sometimes difficult to understand them!

☐ **Hackers** are the cleverest users. They're very good programmers who try to break into computer systems. They can do this because they know _____ weak points in _____ security system. They're usually experts at _____ particular programming language or system. They think it's fun to cause trouble but it's illegal. Some famous hackers are now in prison.

☐ **File Pirates** are only interested in downloading audio and video files (often illegally). They do it all _____ time, so they always want _____ biggest and best hard disks. But they don't listen to or watch 90% of _____ files they get from _____ Internet.

☐ **Hardware Addicts** spend loads of money upgrading their systems. They have _____ best computers. They always want _____ most modern and fastest hardware they can buy. They sometimes build other computers from old parts. They never have enough money for all _____ equipment they want and are always complaining.

☐ **Compulsive Gamers** spend all their time playing computer games. They absolutely have to have _____ very latest version of their favourite game and get _____ highest scores. Many are also hardware addicts and keep upgrading their computers so they can play better and faster games.

☐ **Computer Immigrants** have _____ computer, but rarely use it. They have the worst profile because they don't know how computers work and call technical support for _____ smallest problem. They have _____ e-mail address, but don't check it regularly. Sometimes they send you an e-mail and then phone to ask if you've received it. They're often _____ oldest computer users.

5 Read these comments and match with the different computer users in Exercise 4.

1 *iSCSI usb version 2.0 or FireWire? That's the question.*

2 *Dad, can you lend me two hundred dollars to get a third monitor?*

3 *I'll be outside the shop at 5.30 tomorrow morning. It opens at 9.00.*

4 *I can send you ten more films!*

5 *It's great fun. These companies don't understand how easy it is!!*

6 *Help! I've lost all my files and I only touched one key.*

6 (2.11) Complete the article with *a*, *an* or *the*. Listen, read and check.

Grammar

7 (2.12) Study the yellow phrases. Complete the Grammar box. How is the *-est* ending pronounced? /t/ or /d/? Listen and check.

Superlatives		
Comparative	**Superlative**	**Irregular**
He wants faster hardware.	They want the _____est hardware.	good › _____ bad › _____
These are easier games.	This is the eas_____ game I have.	**Rule**
He's a more passionate user.	They're the _____ passionate users.	We usually use _____ before
She has a bad profile.	They have the w_____ profile.	**superlatives.**
We have good computers.	They have t__ _____ computers.	

> AB, p. 89. Ex. 3 ▶

Listening

8 (2.13) Listen to Rosa and Marco talking about the magazine article. Write T (true) or F (false).

1 Rosa's a computer geek. ____

2 Rosa's computer cost a lot of money. ____

3 Rosa's computer isn't very fast. ____

4 Marco uses his computer for research and shopping. ____

9 (2.14) Listen to the rest of their conversation and complete 1–4 with the correct words.

1 Marco's brother is the _____ _____ gamer he knows.

2 He's got the _____ laptop in the family.

3 He's the _____ gamer in the school.

4 He wants to have the _____ _____ technology.

5 My grandad! He's just the _____ learner.

Speaking

10 In pairs, do you know anybody like these computer users? Which one are you most like? Tell the class.

My younger sister's a computer geek.

11 In threes, make five questions for another group. Use these ideas your own.

Computer Powerful? Old? Modern? Slow?

Games Good? Difficult?

Sat nav Useful? Confusing?

Laptop Light? Sophisticated?

Mobile Small? Attractive? Up-to-date?

12 Swap questions with another group and answer theirs. Report to the class.

We all have modern computers at home.

Have you ever volunteered?

Speaking

1 In threes, race to name an animal beginning with *c, chi, d, f, ha, ho, mo, ra, sn* and *sp*. Then answer the questions. Any coincidences?

1 Have you ever had a pet?

2 How many pets have you had / do you have?

3 Which do you think is the best animal to keep as a pet?

> **Tip**
>
> ... keep *as* a pet NOT ... keep ~~*like* a pet~~.

2 In pairs, answer questions, 1–4. Are your opinions and experiences similar to the rest of the class?

1 Where do you think these photos are from?

2 Have you ever been to any of these places? Do you know anyone who has? Would you like to go there (again)? Why / Why not?

3 Have you ever seen any of these animals? Where exactly?

4 Why do these animals need help?

Reading

3 Quickly read the extract from a TV guide and answer questions, 1–3.

1 Is 'Volunteer with Animals' well known? 2 Do they pay a high salary? 3 Is Mike the name of an elephant?

Making a difference

Volunteer With Animals

Volunteer with Animals is an organization which employs people who want to help animals in different countries. They organise projects in Africa, Asia and Latin America. Most people have never heard of them but they do a lot to protect animals in danger and they need volunteers. Tonight at 8.30, Mike Rogers, who volunteers to work with baby elephants in Kenya, is the star of *Making a difference* an excellent documentary series on TV4. Don't miss it.

4 Match these words and meanings.

an orphanage
the wild
a hunter
die from natural causes
rewarding

where animals live naturally
when something makes you feel good
not killed
home for animals or children with no parents
person who finds and kills animals

Listening

5 (2.15) Listen to the first half of the interview. Complete the sentences with phrases you hear.

1 Mike came to work here _____ .

2 The baby elephants have lost _____ .

3 It's possible that hunters have _____ .

4 The babies need somebody _____ .

6 (2.16) Can you guess what Mike's answers to these questions will be? Listen and check. Were you right?

1 How many elephants have they saved / died?

2 What's his job like?

3 What's the most difficult part of his job?

> **Tip**
> some / any / no one = some / any / nobody

Grammar

7 (2.17) Read the Grammar box then complete the sentences from the interview. Listen, check and repeat.

> **Superlatives and Present perfect**
>
> Use a **superlative** + the Present perfect tense to talk about a special experience.
>
> These sentences often begin with *This / That / It is / was* and include the *first / second / third* time.
>
> This is the b____ thing I h___ e___ done!
>
> It's the f_____ t____ I'__ been to Africa.
>
> I imagine it's the m____ d_____ job you ____ e___ done too!
>
> It's the b____ decision I'__ e___ made.

> AB, p. 90. Ex. 5 ▶

8 (2.18) Where do you think these speakers are? Who do you think they're speaking to? Listen and check.

> 'Yuk! That's the worst thing I've ever tasted!'

> 'Wow! This is the most beautiful animal I've ever seen!'

> 'That was the most comfortable bed I've ever slept in!'

Write another sentence like these for your partner to guess where you are or were.

Speaking

9 (2.19) Name two things you can *make* and two you can *do*. Word Bank 7, p. 70.

10 In pairs, ask and answer questions about three of these things.
Remember a good story to tell the class.

> delicious meal   exciting holiday
> bad film   hard test   difficult decision
> long journey   boring book
> expensive clothes   something crazy

A: It was in Buenos Aires. I went to an Italian restaurant with ... and we had ... .

B: What's the most delicious meal you've ever eaten?

Special memories

Listening

1 (2.20) Listen to people, 1–5. How are they feeling? What are they doing?

(2.21) Word Bank 7, p. 70.

	feeling	doing
1		
2		
3		
4		
5		

2 In pairs, answer the questions about the events in photos A–C.

  1 What are the people doing and how are they feeling?

  2 Why do you think they're feeling like this?

  3 Have you ever been to events like these?

Reading

3 Quickly read Jana and Marc's blogs and match them to an event from Exercise 2.

A day to remember? by Jana

What a brilliant day! There were so many bands from all over the world. OK – tickets were too expensive but it was definitely worth it! It was such a BIG event the whole park was full. And we were lucky with the weather, although it was really boiling. By lunchtime it was so hot that some people had to leave. The crowd were superb although there was some booing when *Coldplay* took ages to come on stage. But when they finally appeared and sang their hits everybody was really happy! There were lots of encores and it finished so late that we missed the last bus home! But we didn't care at all – it was amazing! The best concert I've ever been to!

Running in the rain by Marc

We got to the stadium at 8 a.m. and there were so many events – by the end of the day we were incredibly tired! But the races were really exciting and there was such a lot to see that we didn't know which ones to watch! Our daughter Zara was in the 100 metres. I felt really sorry for her. To start with it was raining so much that the track was a bit like a river! And the Jamaican and American girls she was running against were so fast – she had no chance. She started well but they flew past her and she came last. She was very disappointed and I saw her crying afterwards. But we were very proud of her and it was a great day.

4 In pairs, read the different blogs more carefully. A: read Jana's. B: read Marc's. Answer the questions about your blog. Then tell your partner what happened.

Jana's blog

1 Where did the bands come from?

2 Was it cheap and only half full?

3 Why did some people leave the concert?

4 Why did the crowd boo then cheer and clap?

5 Did Jana catch the last bus home?

Marc's blog

1 Why were they tired by the evening?

2 Why did they go to see these races?

3 Why was it difficult to run?

4 Why did Zara have no chance?

5 How did she feel at the end of the race?

Grammar

5 Study the yellow phrases in both texts. Which two include a noun? Complete the Grammar box with *so* or *such*.

> **so / such ... that**
>
> It was _____ a good concert that Jana will never forget it.
>
> Coldplay played _____ late and _____ long that she missed her bus.
>
> It was _____ a fast race that Zara came last.
>
> Use **so / such ... that** to talk about the result of an action or situation.
>
> Use _____ + an **adjective**.
>
> Use _____ (a) + **adjective** + **noun**.

AB, p. 91. Ex. 1 ▶

6 In pairs, complete the cartoon captions. Were there many different answers in the class?

A

The meal was ...

B

It was ...

C

The film was ...

Listening

7 (2.22) Listen to the news. Circle the correct options. Listen and check. What else can you find out?

1 Tom's *in his car* / *on the street.*

2 They're demonstrating against *pollution* / *a new building.*

3 There's *a very large* / *quite a small* angry crowd.

4 There hasn't been *much* / *any* violence.

Speaking

8 Roleplay: special events.

> A: Tell B about a special event you remember well. Can you talk for a minute? Include the information on the mind map.

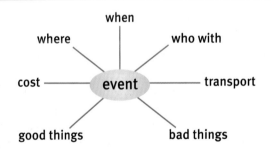

when
where
who with
cost — **event** — transport
good things
bad things

> B: Listen and help A by using the listening phrases and asking questions.

> **Listening phrases**   Yeah / Hmm / Uh-huh
> Right.   I see. Interesting.   Really?
> Go on, tell me more.   Wow!   And then what ...?
> Ow! / Ouch!   Absolutely!   Ah! How nice.
> Oh! Phew!   No! Really?

9 Report back to the class. Who spoke for the longest time? Who was the best listener? Whose story was the most interesting?

Go to **Phrasebook 2** p. 77 ▶   Go to **Essential Grammar 2** p. 114 ▶

② Revision

2A **1** Complete with the correct form of the adjectives and add one extra word.

1 Your exam results were far better than mine.

_My_ exam results were much __*worse*__ than yours. *(bad)*

2 The red printer is €200 so it's cheaper than the blue one, which costs €350.

The blue printer is _____ than ___ red one. *(expensive)*

3 My new laptop is a lot smaller than my old one.

My old laptop was much _____ than my ___ one. *(big)*

4 Julie's a bit younger than me.

I'm ___ little _____ than Julie. *(old)*

5 Is *Twilight* less frightening than *Dracula*?

Is *Dracula* _____ ___ *Twilight*? *(scary)*

2 In pairs, make more comparative sentences about your

[age] [clothes] [family] [hair] [home]

A: *My family is much bigger than yours.*

B: *That's true. And my flat is much smaller than yours!*

2B **3** (2.23) Read about film director, Danny Boyle. Where was he born? What happened in 1994? Then listen and correct six mistakes.

Today, we profile the film director Danny Boyle, who
has become
became one of the UK's greatest film makers. He won many awards over his long career, including the Best Director Oscar for the movie *Slumdog Millionaire*. Boyle was born in Manchester, England, on 12 October 1956 to an English father and an Irish mother. After attending Bangor University, he has directed plays for the theatre, and then began working for the BBC. However, his big break came with *Shallow Grave* in 1994. This was the first of many successful movies, like *Trainspotting*, *The Beach*, and *28 Days Later*. As one of the good film directors around, Boyle has worked with many major movie stars like Leonardo DiCaprio and Ewan McGregor. But he is also an expert at working with actors who are less experienced or young, such as the child stars of *Slumdog Millionaire*, which was set in Bombay (now Mumbai), India.

4 Play HAVE YOU EVER? Get cards from your teacher. Write two more questions. In pairs, ask and answer.

2C **5** Order the sentences and add *enough* or *too*.

1 a / good / isn't / professional / to / footballer / be / he

He isn't good enough to be a professional footballer.

2 not / I'm / marathon / a / fit / run / to

_____ .

3 busy / are / we / to / lunch / have

_____ ?

4 the / today / swim / in / warm / sea / to / it's

_____ .

5 were / tonight / tired / out / go / they / to

_____ .

6 (2.24) Listen and answer.

1 What was the name of the movie?

2 Who enjoyed it more: Carl or Nicola?

3 Who preferred the comic?

7 Listen again. Write T (true) or F (false).

1 At first, Carl thought the film was for children. ___

2 Carl went with his brother. ___

3 Nicola enjoyed the fighting and action in the film. ___

4 Carl thought the film had fewer ideas than the comic. ___

5 Nicola thought parts of the film were just too unbelievable. ___

6 Carl thinks science fiction should be realistic. ___

8 Can you remember six personality adjectives? Word Bank 5, p.68.

Song: *So far away* by Dire Straits

To find the words, google lyric + the name of the song.

To find the video, google video + the name of the song and singer.

2D **9** Read the text. Circle the correct option, 1–7.

Man against machine

Philadelphia, USA 1997: the ⁽¹⁾ *greatest / greater* chess player in the world, Garry Kasparov, played a match against the ⁽²⁾ *most / more* intelligent chess computer ever: IBM's Deep Blue. It was the ⁽³⁾ *most / more* famous chess game of the decade, and the world was waiting to see whether man or machine would win.

However, it wasn't the first game between Kasparov and Deep Blue. In their previous match in 1996, Kasparov was a ⁽⁴⁾ *best / better* player than the computer, and won 4–2. But the experts at IBM spent the next twelve months upgrading their technology and installing new software. So, the Deep Blue of 1997 was ⁽⁵⁾ *fastest / faster* and ⁽⁶⁾ *cleverest / cleverer* than the 1996 machine.

The two competitors played six games and eventually, Deep Blue shocked the world by winning 3½–2½. It was the ⁽⁷⁾ *most / more* incredible victory in chess history!

10 Play THE TALLEST, THE SMALLEST, THE BEST! Get cards from your teacher.

2E **11** Correct the questions.

largest
1 What's the ~~larger~~ animal that you've ever seen?

2 **What's the more beautiful place that you've ever visited?**

3 What's the strangest thing that you're ever eating?

4 **What's the dangerous thing that you've ever done?**

5 What's the funnyest film that you've ever seen?

6 What's the most silliest present that you've ever given anyone?

12 In pairs, ask and answer the questions in Exercise 11.

2F **13** Complete with *so* or *such*.

1 The kids are _____ excited about school that they can't sleep!

2 It was _____ a good concert that I bought all the band's CDs!

3 It was _____ a stupid TV programme that I turned it off after five minutes.

4 Erica looked _____ different with red hair that I didn't recognise her.

5 The sandwiches were _____ disgusting that we couldn't eat them.

6 It was _____ a cool jacket that I had to buy it.

14 Complete with your ideas.

1 A: Why weren't you at work yesterday?
   B: Well, it was such *a hot day that I went to the beach!*

2 A: Do you want to come out tonight?
   B: No. I'm so _____.

3 A: Is it true that you lost your bag last week?
   B: Yes! I was so _____.

4 A: Did you buy your tickets at the station?
   B: No! There was such _____.

5 A: Are you enjoying that book?
   B: It's so _____.

6 A: How was your trip to Italy?
   B: Amazing! It's such _____.

Go to Writing 2 p. 61 ▶

Learn English the modern way

Speaking

1 Answer the survey from a website for English learners. In pairs, compare answers. Any coincidences?

We both started learning English when we were six.

English Learning Survey

By 2050, half the world will speak English! But will they enjoy learning? Complete this online questionnaire to help us find out more about learners' experiences .

1 When did you start learning English?

2 Did you enjoy learning English at first? Why / Why not?

3 What was your first teacher like?

4 Is it better to learn a foreign language when you're very young?

5 Have you picked up most of your English from … ?
- [ ] books
- [ ] the Internet
- [ ] teachers
- [ ] TV / films / music
- [ ] other

6 Which three are the most important for you?
- [ ] grammar
- [ ] listening
- [ ] pronunciation
- [ ] reading
- [ ] speaking
- [ ] vocabulary
- [ ] writing
- [ ] all equally

7 What do you mainly want to use your English for?
- [ ] pleasure
- [ ] work

Reading

2 Quickly read the introduction to an advert from the website and find two reasons why some people can't do a language course.

Learn English the modern way

One of the most popular ways to learn a foreign language globally is by taking classes with a teacher, following a coursebook. But not everybody has enough time to go to a language school. In the past, hours of self study, alone at home, was the only option. Now you can learn another language online, and with other students in the same 'class'! You don't have to travel to study or go abroad. You don't even have to leave your home or office. It's perfect for the 21st century. Welcome to LearnEnglishOnline!

3 Which photo do you think shows the new method? Read the rest of the newsletter to check.

1 What is 'LearnEnglishOnline'?

2 Who is LearnEnglishOnline good for? Why?

How does it work? Well, first you have to register and choose your lesson time. Then you sit _____ at your computer, put _____ your headphones and phone a special number at the right time. Log _____ and link up with a teacher and five other students in different countries. The teacher uses your computer screen like a board to show you videos, explain grammar, ask and answer questions. You can even talk to your virtual classmates. Then, after the lesson, you can print _____ the teacher's notes.

4 (3.1) Complete the text with three different prepositions. Go to Word Bank 8, p. 71.

5 (3.2) Listen to and read the rules. Would you like to learn English like this? Which method is the best for you? Why?

Rules for online learning

1 You **must** **phone** at the right time.

5 You **don't have to** write down anything during the lesson.

2 You **don't have to** learn special computer skills.

6 You **mustn't** interrupt another student.

3 You **mustn't** leave the computer during the lesson.

7 You **mustn't** speak your language 'in class'.

4 You **must** listen and read very carefully.

8 You **have to** do your homework because your teacher will ask you questions.

Grammar

6 Study the yellow phrases in the rules. Which five mean you can't choose (= obligation)? Which two mean you can choose (= no obligation)?

7 Study the cartoons and complete the Grammar box with *must / have to* or *mustn't / don't have to*.

I'm really tired. I must go to bed early tonight.

My class starts at 7.30 a.m so I have to get up early tomorrow.

must / have to	mustn't / don't have to

Use them both for obligations, e.g. rules.

Their positive meanings are very similar, but

+ _____ suggests the idea comes from the speaker.

_____ suggests an action is necessary because of an obligation, e.g. an arrangement

Their negative meanings are very different.

*We **mustn't** speak our language in class.*   *I **don't have to** leave my office to study online.*

− _____ means you can choose.

_____ means you can't choose.

> AB, p. 93. Ex. 3 ▶

8 In pairs, remember the sentences in Exercise 5. Cover the rules and look only at the icons.

9 Look at the cartoons. What must / mustn't you do in each?
Make sentences and add one more example of your own for each location.

Speaking

10 In pairs, list eight things you think people must do in life. Use these ideas or your own.

> *In my country, we say you must plant a tree, have a child and write a book.*

learn (language)	see (man-made wonder)
meet ...	see (natural wonder)
play (sport)	try (food)
read / see (book / film)	visit (city / country)

11 Compare lists with another pair. Do you agree? Choose the top five ideas in the class.

A new life

Listening

1 (3.3) Listen and write down the four questions from a street survey. Match them to the answers. Listen and check. In pairs, answer the questions yourselves.

1 _____

2 _____

3 _____

4 _____

> *Sometimes it's because they want a better lifestyle.*

> *About fifty-fifty I think. It depends on so many things.*

> *Yes. I'd love to. I really want to live in Australia.*

> *A lot of people go to the USA to find work.*

Reading

2 Quickly read the information about a website. Cover the text and answer.

  1 What can you do at this website?

  2 What four things will you learn from each person?

  3 Are there websites like this for your country?

Livingabroad.com

At Livingabroad.com you can read about and listen to people who have moved to different countries. Learn why they moved, the problems they've had, things to avoid and the good points about each place. If you're interested in hearing about life in Italy, Japan or Chile, then just click on the photos to hear interviews with the people.

Listening

3 (3.4) Listen to the first part of the Livingabroad.com interview with Beatriz. Circle the answer.

1 Beatriz was born in *Italy / Mexico*.

2 Now she lives in *America / Italy*.

3 Her husband is *Mexican / American*.

4 She met her husband *seven / eight* years ago.

5 She's been married for *three / five* years.

6 They moved to Italy *two / three* years ago.

7 She started her job *two / six* months ago.

4 (3.5) Listen to the rest of the interview and complete the sentences. Shadow read the audioscript on page 109 to check your answers. Note the links.

  1 They now live in _____.

  2 They lived in _____ for the first year.

  3 It was very _____.

  4 They both like _____.

  5 English is _____ for her than Danny.

  6 Things are more _____ than in Mexico.

  7 Italy is a _____ country.

  8 They want to stay as long as _____.

Grammar

5 Complete the Grammar box with sentences from the interview. Then study the timeline and complete the rules with *for* or *since*.

Present perfect to join the past and the present

➕ I'_____ worked for a clothing company for six months.

➖ We have _____ lived here all the time.

❓ How long _____ you _____ married?

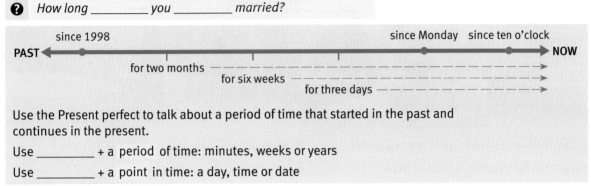

Use the Present perfect to talk about a period of time that started in the past and continues in the present.

Use _____ + a period of time: minutes, weeks or years

Use _____ + a point in time: a day, time or date

AB, p. 94. Ex. 1 ▶

6 Which of these time expressions can complete sentences 1 and 2?

2005   eight years   two months   three weeks   Monday   4th March   my birthday party

1 I've known Rita since ...

2 Mike's been a teacher for ...

Pronunciation

7 Read the questions out loud. Link *long* and *have / has* . Notice the silent *h* . In pairs, answer the questions.

How long have you lived here?

How long have you known me?

How long has our teacher worked here?

How long've you had those shoes?

8 Look again at the interview on page 109. Say all the links. Complete this rule with vowel and consonant.

Rules

Link words ending with a _____ sound if the next word begins with a _____ sound.

(3.6) Word Bank 12, p. 75.

Speaking

9 Work in small groups. Write four questions you'd like to ask the rest of your group. Use these verbs and ideas (or your own).

How long have you ... ?

have	short hair / mobile / pet / favorite jeans
be	current job / at this school / into (yoga)
live	alone / with your family / partner / in this town
know	your partner / teacher / classmates

10 Ask your questions and remember the answers. Read out your sentences for the class to guess who you are talking about.

A: 'This person has only been at this school for ten days.'

B: That's Veronique!

How good is your vocabulary?

Speaking

1 (3.7) How many different phrases do you remember with *get*? Word Bank 2, p. 65.

2 In pairs, answer the questions about the games in the photos.

1 What do you think you have to do in these games?

2 Are these games for children, adults or both?

3 Have you got / do you play games like this?

4 What's your favourite game?

Reading

3 Read this article from an English learners' website and find three ways students can learn new words. How do you play 'Password'?

PASSWORD Nobody knows every word in a language, not even native speakers. There are far too many words, especially technical ones which hardly anybody uses!

By now, you probably know around 2000 English words actively and many more passively too. To speak well, learners generally need an active vocabulary of about 5,000 words, so you're making very good progress.

To increase your vocabulary more quickly, you can read a lot or use special study techniques. For example, some learners write down all the new words they read or hear each day and try to learn them! But there are fun ways too, like word games, crosswords and other puzzles and popular board games like Scrabble.

Another less well-known board game which is great for language learning is 'Password'. In this game you have to race to give definitions of words and phrases, for your partners to guess them.

4 Here are some cards from Password. Which words are they defining?

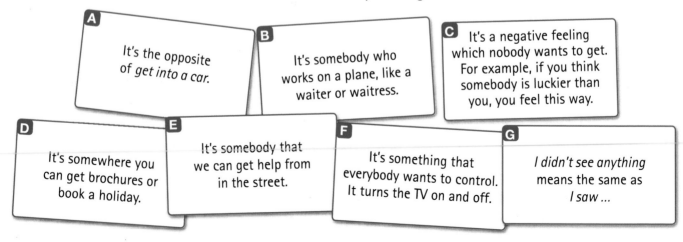

A It's the opposite of *get into a car*.

B It's somebody who works on a plane, like a waiter or waitress.

C It's a negative feeling which nobody wants to get. For example, if you think somebody is luckier than you, you feel this way.

D It's somewhere you can get brochures or book a holiday.

E It's somebody that we can get help from in the street.

F It's something that everybody wants to control. It turns the TV on and off.

G I didn't see anything means the same as I saw ...

Grammar 1

5 Complete the Grammar box with *anybody, everybody, nobody* or *somebody*.

anybody / everybody / nobody / somebody

A My teacher said _____ knows every word in a language.

B _____ wants to speak English well!

C A translator is _____ who works with languages.

D I can't find _____ who knows the answer.

anybody / **any**where / **any**thing
= not a person / place or thing

everybody / **every**where / **every**thing
= all people / places / things

nobody / **no**where / **no**thing
= not one person / place / thing

somebody / **some**where / **some**thing
= a definite person / place or thing

AB, p. 95. Ex. 2 ▶

Grammar 2

6 Complete the cards with *who, which* or *that*. Then complete the Grammar box.

A It's a large, black and white animal _____ lives in Africa.

B It's somebody _____ drives a taxi.

C It's something _____ wakes you up in the morning.

who / which / that

Use _____ or *that* to define people.
Use _____ or _____ to define things.

AB, p. 95. Ex. 3 ▶

Listening

7 (3.8) Listen to Karin and Sven and complete her sentences with *which / that* or *who*. How does she feel by the end of their conversation?

1 Johnny's the guy _____ sold me my new bike.

2 It's a new café _____ has opened in the High Street.

3 Password is a new game _____ I got last week.

8 (3.9) Listen to Karin and Sven playing Password. Complete the phrases.

You'll never _____ it!

I know what you _____.

It's on the _____ of my tongue.

It begins _____ 'C'!

Sorry, it's _____!

Do you _____ up?

Pronunciation

9 (3.10) Listen and read. Notice the words that are stressed. Then practise repeating them.

Sven: *It's **something** that you **use** for **opening bottles** of **wine**.*

Karin: *It's on the **tip** of my **tongue**.*

Tip
You don't usually stress words like *a, you, for, of,* or *my*.

Speaking

10 Get cards from your teacher and play Password.

A holiday with a difference

Speaking

1 (3.11) How did you get here today? Did it take long? What did you see on the way? Word Bank 9, p. 72.

2 Imagine what the people in photos 1–4 did on holiday? Which holiday would you prefer to go on?

Reading

3 Read a British magazine article as fast as you can and answer.

1 Which photo goes with the article?

2 What's the Rabbit Run?

3 Are the roads better in France or the UK?

4 Is Jenna's mum happier about where she's going next?

An exciting week.
By Jenna Craven.

My best holiday ever was last year! My mate Nick knows I love cars and driving, and he invited me to go with him on the Rabbit Run. I know – I didn't know what it was either! It's a car tour through five or six European countries along public roads. The cars that go on the tour are fantastic and very quick! Nick was the main driver and I gave him directions. But sometimes I drove. His car's an Audi and it was an amazing experience! After a day's driving you stay in wonderful hotels, meet some crazy people and have a great time. Some people say it's a race. But it isn't really. Yes – the people who go on the Rabbit Run love driving fast and there are some great roads in Europe for driving as fast as you want! The roads in the UK are definitely not as good as the ones in France and Germany. But really it's a chance to visit a lot of different countries. You see some wonderful scenery and talk a lot about cars! And we didn't drive too fast – really!

This year I'm going climbing in the Andes with some friends. Apart from the flight of course, it's not nearly as expensive as the Rabbit Run and I won't stay in such luxury hotels. Climbing isn't as exciting as car racing but it can be just as dangerous and I'm sure my mum will still worry just the same! But I love holidays that are a bit different. In my opinion it's much better than just sitting on a beach in the sun!

4 (3.12) Cover the text. In pairs, try to remember ten things that Jenna likes and one thing she doesn't like. Listen and check.

Grammar

5 Study the yellow phrases. Complete the Grammar box.

> **as ... as**
>
> Jenna's mum will ____ just ____ worried ____ she was last year!
>
> Climbing isn't ____ expensive ____ driving, but it ____ just ____ dangerous.
>
> Use *(not) as ... as* to say something is (not) the same as something else.
>
> AB, p. 96. Ex. 2 ▶

Pronunciation

6 (3.13) Listen and check. How is as ... as pronounced?

7 In threes, compare these things now and a few years ago.

the weather   fashion (clothes, music)

technology   food and water

transport and tourism   free-time activities

A: In my country, winters aren't as cold now as before.

B: That's right, and it sometimes rains much more than before too.

C: There aren't as many tourists as there were a few years ago!

Listening

8 (3.14) Look at the map. Listen to Jenna directing Nick to a hotel. Start at **X** and follow the directions.

(3.15) Word Bank 9, p. 72.

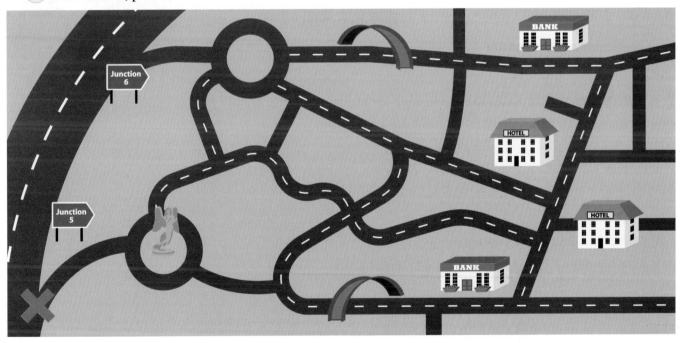

9 Listen again and choose the correct words to complete the sentences.

1 *Take / Make* the next junction off the motorway.

2 Go *along / down* the hill.

3 Turn *right / to the right* at the crossroads.

4 Go *through / under* the bridge.

5 Turn left *on / at* the bank.

6 It's the second *turning / exit* on the right.

7 There's the hotel *on / in* the right.

Speaking

10 In pairs, choose a place on the map and direct your partner to it. Race the class and see who gets there first.

High earners

Speaking

1 In teams, race to think of two irregular past simple verbs that rhyme with *blue*, *red*, *hot*, *cold* and *short*. One point for each. Word Bank 13, p. 76.

2 In pairs, match photos 1–8 to their names. Match each person to the profession(s) below. What else do you know about them?

- [ ] Johnny Cash _____
- [ ] Kurt Cobain _____
- [ ] Albert Einstein _____
- [ ] John Lennon _____
- [ ] Marilyn Monroe _____
- [ ] Elvis Presley _____
- [ ] Charles M. Schultz _____
- [ ] Andy Warhol _____

an actor / actress	a painter
a cartoonist	a photographer
a guitarist	a scientist
a musician	a singer

Listening

3 (3.16) Do the quiz using people from Exercise 2. Listen and complete. Answer the last question you hear.

Welcome to this year's Top Celebrity Earners – who are dead!

Yes, here we list the famous stars who continue to make the most millions after they've died. But before we tell you this year's winners, try our quiz to find last year's Top Celebrity Earners.

	name	died	earned
1 Who recorded 'Heartbreak hotel' in 1958?	_____	1977	_____
2 Who wrote, sang and played guitar with Nirvana and shot himself aged 27?	_____	1994	_____
3 Which ex-Beatle 'imagined all the people' and 'gave peace a chance'?	_____	_____	40m
4 Who created Charlie Brown and drew the Peanuts cartoons?	_____	2000	32m
5 Who decided E=mc² and was the best-known scientist of the 20th century?	_____	1955	_____
6 Who had white hair, glasses and painted pop art pictures of Marilyn Monroe in the 60s?	_____	1987	13.7m
7 Which country and western singer sang in prisons and always wore black clothes?	_____	_____	7m
8 Who was the world's top sex symbol, made 29 films and died at 36?	_____	1962	6.4m

Grammar

4 Label the subject and object in this sentence. Then match questions 1 and 2 to the subject or object. How are they different?

Elvis Presley recorded 553 songs.

1 Who recorded the songs?

2 How many songs did Elvis record?

5 Circle the subjects and underline the objects in the eight questions in the quiz opposite.

6 Complete the Grammar box with these letters: A, I, V, S or Q.

Subject and Object questions

	Rules	Example
A = auxiliary verb	**1** For *Yes / No* questions use ___A___ + ____ + ____	*Do you like rock n roll?*
I = infinitive verb		
V = verb in correct tense	**2** For object questions, use ____ + ____ + ____ + ____	*Who do you like listening to?*
S = subject		
Q = question	**3** For subject questions, use ____ + ____	*Who likes classical music?*

AB, p. 97. Ex. 3 ▶

7 In pairs, ask and answer the Example questions above. Any differences?

Pronunciation

8 (3.17) Listen and complete the expressions. Mark the links.

1 That's an easy one.

2 _____ was _____ ago.

3 _____ you _____ _____ _____ clue?

4 I've got _____ _____.

5 _____ heard _____ him!

6 That's _____.

Speaking

9 In small teams, make a quiz about modern celebrities. Write five questions. Swap quizzes with another team and try to answer the questions.

1 *Who sang / played … ?*

2 *What films did … make?*

Take a break!

Speaking

1 Look at the photo for ten seconds, cover it and, in pairs, answer the questions.

 1 Describe the people in the photo.

 2 What's happening and why?

 3 Guess where the girls are going.

Reading

2 Four more indefinite articles are missing in this dictionary definition. Can you find where they go?

> **A gap year** noun (BrE) A year that young person spends working / and / or travelling, often between leaving school and starting university. Also for older person who wants break from work.: *I'm planning to take gap year and go back-packing in India.*

3 Read and complete the website homepage with *for, off, out,* or *up* (× 3). Word Bank 10, p. 73.

> Fancy a break from studying or from work before you give (1) _____ and retire? Want to travel and learn a bit about the world? Maybe take (2) _____ a new hobby or pick (3) _____ another language? Perhaps you need time to decide what course or career to study at university? Or perhaps you just want a change?
>
> At gapyearadvice.com we can help you. If you decide a gap year is for you then we can help you find (4) _____ about health and safety issues before you set (5) _____ . We can also help you look (6) _____ work abroad and plan your special year carefully.
>
> Click (COMMENTS) to read the messages left by visitors to this site.

4 Would you like to go on a gap year? Why / Why not?

5 In threes, read the texts. A: read Anton. B: read Beat. C: read Chris. Is the text positive about gap years?

Anton

I <u>set off</u> to Australia for my gap year. I'm really glad I went! I worked in a hotel there and I learned so much! I learned how to organise things in the restaurant and kitchens. I also had to <u>deal with</u> the customers and sort out their problems. Of course, I also learned to <u>look after</u> myself and that was very important – no mum or dad to do everything for me! I earned a lot of money too and that helped <u>pay for</u> my university course when I <u>went back</u> home.

Beat

I'm afraid I'm definitely against this idea of taking a year off your studies. I've heard of students who go travelling and then never <u>go back</u> to studying – like my cousin. She <u>gave up</u> the whole idea. They like earning the money and seeing new places and university is boring after that. I'm <u>looking forward to</u> starting university next year. I really want a degree and a good job!

Chris

I've worked for this company for about ten years and in that time I've employed a lot of students after university. In my opinion it's a great idea to take a gap year. Teenagers <u>grow up</u> a lot when they have to work and look after themselves. They also <u>pick up</u> a lot of useful skills. When I'm <u>looking for</u> a new employee I want someone who's got more than just a qualification.

6 In threes, decide which person, Anton, Beat, or Chris, thinks a gap year ... ? Circle A, B or C.

1	isn't a good idea	A	B	C
2	is a good experience	A	B	C
3	helps you get a job later	A	B	C
4	means you can earn a lot of money	A	B	C
5	helps you learn useful skills	A	B	C

> **Tip**
> I also learned to *look after myself*.
> NOT ~~look after me~~.

Grammar

7 (3.18) Read the Grammar box. Which phrasal verbs in Exercise 5 are separable? Which are inseparable? Word Bank 10, p. 73.

Phrasal verbs (PVs)

*I **gave up** smoking last year.*   ***Look after** yourself.*   *Oh no. I've **run out of** milk.*

PVs are *verbs + prepositions* that combine to give a certain meaning. This meaning isn't always clear from the meanings of the two individual words.

Phrasal verbs and objects

1 Some PVs don't have an object.	*We **set off** early in the morning.*
2 Separable: Some PVs can have the object either: **after** the preposition **between** the verb and preposition	*I **gave up** smoking last year.* *I **gave** smoking **up** last year.*
3 Inseparable: Some PVs can ONLY have the object **after** the preposition.	*I'm **looking after** the kids.* **NOT** *I'm **looking** the kids **after**.*

> AB, p. 98. Ex. 1 ▶

8 In pairs, tell your partner these things. Any coincidences?

1 some information you found out recently
2 a hobby or sport you took up in the last few years
3 the last word you looked up in the dictionary
4 something you've given up or want to give up
5 something you had to look for recently

Listening

9 (3.19) Jack's planning to take a year off. Circle all the things he talks about.

1 Jack wants to go to *North America / Asia / South America*.
2 He wants to *stay in one place / visit many places / find a job*.
3 He wants to travel by *plane / train / bus / bike / car*.
4 He needs to find out about *the weather / places to stay / health insurance / currencies*.

10 In pairs, plan a gap year for a student coming to your country. Whose gap year plan in the class is

1 the most interesting?
2 the most useful?

> *First he can work for a few months in ... to save some money. He can get a job as ... . If he does that he can pick up the language ... .*

> *Then he can travel round the country. I think he should go to ... and find out about the people and the customs.*

Go to **Phrasebook 3** p. 78 ▶   Go to **Essential Grammar 3** p. 116 ▶

3A 1 (3.20) Listen and match 1–4 with a situation. Then listen again and complete.

1	a car problem	☐	Mother's Day
☐	going to the bank	☐	travelling abroad

1 A: Every time we get to 60 km an hour, it starts making that noise. I _____ do something about it.

B: Well, you _____ have to _____ to a garage. My brother's a mechanic. He'll look at it for you.

2 A: You _____ to tell the boss every time you leave the office.

B: But the bank closes at 2.30 and I have _____ pay this now.

A: No, it closes at 5. You don't _____ to _____ now. You can go later.

3 A: _____ we have _____ have a visa to go there?

B: Yes, and we _____ organise it before we leave. I'll do it tomorrow.

4 A: I _____ forget to get my mum a card. I didn't get her anything last year and I was in big trouble.

B: I _____ have _____ get anything for mine. She doesn't think it's important.

2 In threes, ask and answer *What do you have to do this week?*

A: *What do you have to do this week?*

B: *I must email my cousin.*

C: *I have to write an essay for college.*

3B 3 Complete with the correct form of the verbs and *for* or *since*.

1 Nobody <u>has spoken</u> to Martina <u>since</u> last week. (*speak*)

2 I _____ Vassilis _____ all my life. (*know*)

3 Daniela _____ with us _____ January last year. (*live*)

4 He looks terrible. He _____ _____ yesterday. (*eat*)

5 Piotr _____ for IBM _____ about five years. (*work*)

4 In pairs, complete with your own answers. Write two more for your partner to complete.

1 I haven't seen _____ this year.

2 I haven't eaten _____ since I was a child.

3 I've known _____ all my life.

4 I haven't been to _____ for a long time.

5 _____ .

6 _____ .

5 In groups, compare your answers to Exercise 4 and give more information.

My sister has gone to the USA to study. That's why I haven't seen her.

3C 6 Replace *that* with *who* or *which*.

I have to tell you about my holidays. I was in a tourist resort [1] ~~that~~ *which* is famous for water sports. When I arrived, there were two people there. There was a woman [2] **that** was putting equipment on the boat, and a man [3] **that** was the captain. I gave the woman my bags. She took them but looked at me in a strange way. Then we waited, because there were other tourists [4] **that** were late. I asked the woman questions about the trip [5] **that** we were doing but the answers [6] **that** she gave me were very bad. She didn't know anything!

We arrived at an island and everyone jumped into the sea. The captain was the only person [7] **that** was still on the boat. The woman was swimming. When she got back, I said "You're the guide, but you haven't told us anything about the island [8] **that** we're visiting!" The woman said, "But I'm a tourist too!"

7 📄 Play VOCABULARY RACE! Get cards from your teacher. The first pair to answer all the question wins!

3D **8** In pairs, write sentences with *as ... as* to compare

1 (your family) _____ .

2 (hobbies) _____ .

3 (last holiday) _____ .

9 In pairs, compare holidays you had as a child with your holidays now. Find five differences.

When I was younger, my parents took me on holidays in my country. Now I go abroad on my own.

3E **10** (3.21) Complete the questions and circle the answers. Then listen and check.

What do you know about Portugal?

1 What _happened_ (happen) ___in___ Lisbon ___on___ November 1, 1755?

  a an earthquake

  b a hurricane

2 Whose family originally _____ (come) _____ Portugal?

  a Lewis Carroll

  b Harold Pinter

3 _____ many people _____ (live) _____ Portugal today?

  a about 6 million

  b about 11 million

4 Which Portuguese football team _____ (win) the Champions League _____ 2004?

  a FC Porto

  b Sporting

5 Who _____ (die) _____ 1523 when he was trying _____ travel round _____ world?

  a Ferdinand Magellan

  b Vasco da Gama

3F **11** In pairs, look at Word Bank 10. Cover and test. How many phrasal verbs can you remember?

12 Complete with the correct particles.

1 I've given _____ drinking coffee. I feel much better.

2 We need a babysitter to look _____ the children tonight.

3 I'm looking _____ my keys. Have you seen them?

4 I'm just going to put _____ some make up before we go out.

5 Don't throw those bottles _____ . We can recycle them.

6 The kids are growing _____ so fast. Tomas is already 14!

7 I'm sorry, Professor Wei isn't here. Can you call _____ ?

13 Write three sentences about yourself using phrasal verbs from Word Bank 10. Leave a gap for the phrasal verb for your partner to guess.

A: *I'm _____ to seeing my boyfriend tonight.*

B: *looking forward*

14 Can you remember how many consonant sounds there are? How many are voiced and unvoiced? Word Bank 12, p. 75.

Song: *It's my party* by Bryan Ferry

To find the words, google lyric + the name of the song.

To find the video, google video + the name of the song and singer.

Go to **Writing 3** p. 62 ▶

Memorable moments

Speaking

1 (4.1) What's happening in pictures A–E? Which person is ... ? Word Bank 8, p. 71.

I think he's feeling proud of washing the car because....

embarrassed (about) interested (in) jealous (of)
proud (of) upset (about)

Reading

2 You're going to read a webpage about childhood memories. First, match questions 1–5 and pictures A–E. Then, in pairs, answer the questions. Which of you has the clearer memories?

How good is your memory? How much do you remember about ...

1 your first class at school?

2 a book or game you really enjoyed as a child?

3 the first way you earned money?

4 something naughty you did at school?

5 a sickness or injury you had?

3 In threes, each read one answer from the webpage. Which picture is it and which question is it answering? Tell your group about the person's memories.

A

My memory isn't usually good but I remember my first class really well! Our teacher was a kind young woman but I can't think of her name. I remember sitting next to a girl called Alicia and she had long blond hair. She was very pretty and clever too. She answered all the questions and the teacher always smiled at her. I was very jealous of poor Alicia. I was short and dark and I couldn't do sports or paint but Alicia could do all those things. There was another kid I liked, a boy called Marco. I didn't mind sitting next to him because he helped me a lot! Also, he was bad at singing and I was better than him. Things like that are important when you're six! I met Marco again a few years ago. He's a top scientist now! But I have no idea what happened to Alicia – she's probably a film star.

Rosa, Mexico, **19**

B

One of my clearest memories is also one of my worst! My teacher caught me cheating in an exam! I was about 11 and had to pass to go up to the next school. That was my first important exam and I was so worried about failing. Doing the exam was terrible. My mouth was dry and my hands were shaking. I was desperate. I remember sitting there for an hour and a half with an empty head. I couldn't answer any of the questions. So, I copied my friend's answers. I felt awful about it but then it got even worse! The teacher saw me and she sent me home. I was so embarrassed that I felt like crying. Of course, I failed. I never cheated again. That was a moment I'd really like to forget but I don't think I ever will!

Matt, UK, **23**

C

I can still remember that afternoon clearly! It was my best friend Ana's birthday and we were six years old. She was having a party and I remember getting a new dress and shoes – they were pink! I can also remember buying her a Barbie doll and feeling jealous because I wanted to keep it for myself. Anyway, we went round to her house before the party so my mum could help. Getting ready for the party was great fun. And helping her grandma with the birthday cake was wonderful too. But being sick just after the party started wasn't very nice! I ate too many cakes and biscuits. I had to leave early and I cried all afternoon. I was sick for days! I'll never forget it!

Magda, Poland, **25**

Grammar

4 Match rules 1–3 and examples, A–C, in the Grammar box. Then match the yellow examples in the texts to the rules.

> **-ing form**
>
> **Use the -ing form**
> 1 **as the subject of a sentence.** ___
> 2 **after prepositions.** ___
> 3 **after certain verbs** ___
>
> A *I enjoyed reading the Harry Potter books.*
> B *I wasn't good at swimming.*
> C *Cleaning cars was the first way I earned money.*
>
> Seven important verbs followed by *-ing* are:
> *enjoy, feel like, finish, give up, mind, remember, suggest*

AB, p. 100. Ex. 2 ▶

5 Complete these sentences with an *-ing* form. Compare with a partner. Any big differences?

1 As a child I spent my evenings _____

2 At secondary school I was good at _____

3 I really don't enjoy _____

4 _____ is one of my favourite activities.

5 _____ is something I've always wanted to do.

Listening

6 (4.2) Match beginnings 1–6 with the best ending a–f. Listen and check.

1 Perhaps the best thing about being a child

2 The most difficult thing about secondary school

3 The hardest thing about studying at university

4 I think the worst thing about having to work

5 Maybe the nicest thing about being in love

6 The most enjoyable thing about retiring

> a is not having enough free time.
>
> b was not having to worry about anything.
>
> c was trying to study after not sleeping all night.
>
> d is feeling so positive all the time.
>
> e will be having more time to do my own things.
>
> f was having to study too many subjects.

Speaking

7 In pairs, write different endings for the sentences in Exercise 6. Swap with another pair and match them to the right sentences.

8 In pairs, write three more questions for the webpage in Exercise 2. Ask other students and tell the class the most interesting answers.

What's your earliest memory?

4B Looking good

Speaking

1 (4.3) List three things people can do to look younger. Word Bank 7, p. 70.

Avoid the sun, eat healthy food ...

Listening

2 (4.4) Listen to three radio adverts about ways to look younger. Which one is American English? Then match the adverts to photos 1–3.

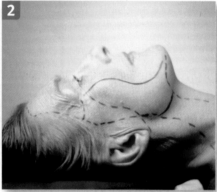

3 Listen again and complete the information. Which do you think is the best advert?

A

Name of place:

_____

What they do:

_____

How long ago did they start?

over _____

How much does a first visit

cost? _____

B

Name of first product:

_____

When should you use it?

_____

Name of second product:

_____

Cost: _____

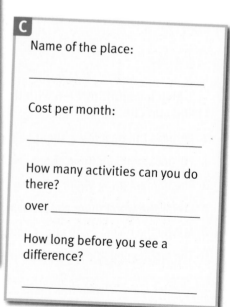

C

Name of the place:

_____

Cost per month:

_____

How many activities can you do there?

over _____

How long before you see a difference?

_____

Pronunciation

4 Go to page 110. Listen again and shadow read the adverts.

 1 Is /ə/ stressed?
 2 Can you hear any difference in the American pronunciation of the letter *r*?
 3 Do you know which verbs the underlined nouns come from?

Grammar

5 (4.5) Complete the Grammar box with *will*, *won't* or *might*. Cross out two more wrong words in the rules. Listen, check and repeat the examples.

will and might

+
You _____ look years younger.

It _____ rain tomorrow – you never know.

−
I promise you _____ regret it.

It _____ / _____ not rain tomorrow – for a change!

?
_____ I both feel and look healthier?

What _____ you look like in 20 years' time?

Use *will / won't* to make ~~plans~~ / predictions / promises about the present / future when we *are / aren't* very sure.

Use *might (not)* if something in the future is / isn't very sure.

AB, p. 101. Ex. 2 ▶

Tip

The verbs *may* and *might* are often used for the same situations – when you are not sure or have not decided yet.

I may be late for our next class.

Pronunciation

6 (4.6) Listen and repeat sentences 1–4. Be careful with the letter *l*.

1 Will you have more muscle?

2 They'll give you the best possible advice.

3 We'll really help you look and feel like a new person!

4 Lovely little ladies like lovely little lemons.

7 Do you agree? Why / Why not? In pairs, discuss.

In 20 years' time …

1 everyone will have cosmetic surgery.

2 most people will be obese.

3 men will use as many beauty products as women.

4 nobody will smoke.

5 restaurants won't serve alcohol.

6 cars won't use petrol.

Speaking

8 In small groups, write a short TV advert to advertise one of A–D (or choose your own idea). Write one sentence for each point.

A

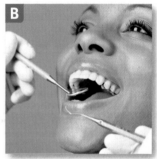
B

C

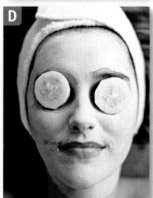
D

1 name

2 reasons for going / choosing / using

3 promises and predictions

4 cost

5 what to do next – phone / email / visit / apply

9 Read or act your advert to the class. Award your class Oscars for the

1 funniest.

2 most unusual.

3 most believable.

Friends for life?

Listening

1 (4.7) Sue and Deb are talking about a questionnaire in a magazine. Listen and complete statements, 1–5. Can you remember Deb's answers? Does she agree? Listen and check.

Friends	agree	disagree
1 _____ friends are the best friends.	A	D
2 It's better to have _____ really good friends than _____ quite good ones!	A	D
3 You can't _____ friendship.	A	D
4 A real friend is someone who will _____ for you.	A	D
5 Friendship is _____ than love.	A	D

Pronunciation

2 Turn to page 110. Listen again and shadow read. Pronounce the links and don't pronounce the crossed out letters. Which consonant is often 'silent' ?

3 In pairs, answer the questionnaire. Are your answers similar to Deb's?

Reading

4 Quickly read the advert opposite for a new website. What's it for?

1 making new friends around the world

2 finding old friends

3 stories about the end of friendship

5 (4.8) Read the advert again and choose the correct prepositions. Word Bank 11, p. 74.

1 from / with   5 together / in

2 to / in   6 in / on

3 of / about   7 onto / into

4 with / to   8 to / from

Friends for life

As we get older we often lose touch (1) _____ old friends. We change schools or jobs, move (2) _____ different towns – or abroad. Daily texts become monthly emails, then these change into the occasional card and then soon we lose contact completely. Perhaps our lives get too busy or addresses and phone numbers get lost.

But sometimes we think (3) _____ these old friends and want to know what's happened (4) _____ them. Here at *Friends for life* we try to bring old friends (5) _____. Would you like to get (6) _____ touch with an old friend? If you send us some details we'll do our best to find him or her for you. And if we find them, we'll send them your contact details. So far, we've put thousands of people back in touch. If we don't find your friend, we won't charge you. But we're optimistic! If you go (7) _____ our website, you'll see comments (8) _____ lots of satisfied customers! Let us help you!

6 In threes, think of five reasons for losing touch. What will the website do for people who have lost touch? Have you ever used the Internet to try to find an old friend?

Grammar

7 Study the yellow verbs in the text. Complete the sentences with the two verbs in brackets. Then read the Grammar box and complete the rules with three of the words.

If we _____ your friend, we _____ you in contact (find, put).

If we _____ your friend, you _____ pay anything (not find, not have to).

first conditional

impossible   possible   present   verb

To form the first conditional use *if* + _____ and *will / won't* + _____.

Use the first conditional to talk about a _____ future situation.

AB, p. 102. Ex. 2 ▶

Listening

8 Match cartoons 1–6 with a verb from the box.

☐ help   ☐ lend   ☐ lie   ☐ share   ☐ tell the truth   ☐ tell / keep secrets

9 (4.9) Listen to a street survey about friendship. Which picture don't they talk about?

Speaking

10 In pairs, play 'Telepathy'.

1 Think of an ending for each of these sentences.

2 Guess what your partner's ending will be.

3 How many guesses did you get right?

If I eat too much chocolate …

We won't destroy the world if …

I might go to bed early tonight if …

You won't live very long if …

If it rains this weekend …

If I fall in love tomorrow …

If you turn off your computer …

If you lend me $100 …

I might go to the cinema tonight if …

I'll speak English better if …

I won't work tomorrow if …

You won't be popular if …

4D I earn too much!

Speaking

1 In pairs, go to Word Bank 5, p.68. Cover the words and try to remember all the adjectives in two minutes. Then close your books and try to list an adjective beginning with each letter of the alphabet. Which pair has the longest list?

2 Read the newspaper headline. Why do you think Andy said this?

> ### Andy says: I earn too much and I shouldn't get a promotion!

1 He is lazy and doesn't do his job well.

2 He thinks other people are as good as he is.

3 He has lied about his qualifications.

4 He wears nice clothes and says the right things but isn't very good at his job.

Listening

3 (4.10) Listen to a TV interview with Andy to check your guess. Does Nicole think her own salary is fair?

4 (4.11) Listen to the rest of the interview. Why does Andy think he gets more money?

5 In pairs, circle what's (S) the same and what's (D) different for Andy and his friend. Listen again to the complete interview to check. Do you agree with Andy? Why / Why not? Is this a common problem in your country?

Company	S	D	Hours	S	D	Qualified	S	D
Office	S	D	Organised	S	D	Years in the company	S	D
Work	S	D	Computer work	S	D	Salary	S	D
Position	S	D						

Grammar

6 Complete the Grammar box with information from the interview.

much, a lot, a bit + comparative

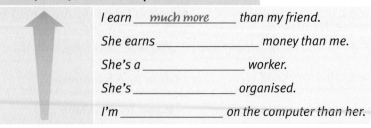

I earn ___*much more*___ than my friend.

She earns _____ money than me.

She's a _____ worker.

She's _____ organised.

I'm _____ on the computer than her.

Use *much*, *a lot* and *a bit* to compare bigger and smaller differences.

AB, p. 103. Ex. 2 ▶

Pronunciation

7 (4.12) Listen and check the Grammar box. Circle the stressed words in each sentence. Why do we stress these words? Listen and repeat the sentences.

> **Tip**
>
> We usually stress the important words: the ones which carry the meaning.
>
> These words are usually slower and louder than the rest.

8 In pairs, compare these things. Which do you prefer and why?

| hypermarkets and local supermarkets |

| going camping and staying in a hotel |

| the weather this month and last |

| your country and the country nearest to yours |

| flying and travelling by bus |

| the best and worst jobs / courses you've ever done |

| British and American English |

| men and women |

Hypermarkets are MUCH bigger.

And they sell a LOT more things.

But they're TOO big and really unfriendly.

Reading

9 Read and match four of sentences 1–8 to cartoons A–D. In pairs, decide if you agree or disagree and say why.

1 Women are a bit more intuitive than men. ___
2 Men talk a lot more quickly than women. ___
3 Women talk much more than men. ___
4 Men are less complimentary than women. ___
5 Men interrupt a lot more than women. ___
6 Men and women usually laugh at the same things. ___
7 Men ask for help much more than women. ___
8 Women are a lot more self-critical than men. ___

10 🗋 Get a card from your teacher to read and compare answers. Tell the class if you were surprised by anything you read.

4E Changes

1 In pairs, how many consonant sounds are there in English? How many can you remember? Word Bank 12, p. 75.

A

Speaking

2 In pairs, compare photos A and B of the same city.

1 Which one is older? How much older?

2 What has changed in the more recent photo?

3 Imagine how life is different now for the people who live there.

Reading

3 Work in threes. Look at the photos and read the captions. Imagine five big differences in lifestyle for each of them.

Ken, a 15 year old Chinese boy whose family moved from the country to the city.

Boris and Olga, a couple from Russia who have retired to Spain.

Ahmet, an ex-top lawyer in Istanbul who gave up his job to become a gardener.

4 Read the article. Each student in the group reads about one person. Tell the group if your ideas were right.

Dramatic changes!

For many of us, life continues in the same way, in the same place, year after year. But sometimes dramatic decisions can change our lives completely. Ken, Olga and Ahmet write about their personal dramas.

Ken

My family moved to Beijing a few years ago when my father got a building job here for the Olympic Games. Life in such a big, modern city is very, very different from our old village. I used to walk to school and it took me ten minutes. Now I go by bus and some days it can take an hour or more because there's so much traffic! In the country we used to live in a small house and knew everybody on our street. Here we live in an enormous block of apartments and don't know anybody! Everybody is so busy! Of course, in our village there weren't many good shops or places to go in the evening but life in Beijing is much more expensive. I suppose life used to be much quieter, healthier and slower but it was definitely a lot more boring!

Olga

Ages ago, we decided to retire somewhere hot and in 2007 we sold our house in Russia and bought a lovely flat just outside Valencia, near the sea. Our lives here are completely different. It's almost impossible to compare! The weather is much better of course, we're outside nearly all the time and wear completely different clothes. We eat much more fresh food and we don't get colds as often as we used to! We lived in Vladivostok, a polluted city, and that wasn't good for our health either. We didn't use to have much free time because we both worked such a lot. Life used to be very stressful. We're making lots of new friends too. It's wonderful.

Ahmet

I used to be a lawyer in Istanbul, the biggest, craziest city in Europe. Well, two thirds of it is in Europe! I've always lived just outside the city in a lovely small town, so I used to have to commute through the traffic daily. Every day was long, busy and very stressful and I never really stopped working. Finally, last year, I decided to give it up and now I work as a gardener in my town. People thought I was crazy because I used to earn a great salary but there are far more important things in life! I didn't use to get any fresh air and now I'm outside all the time! Life is much calmer too and I enjoy each minute more. It was the best decision I've ever made.

Listening

5 (4.13) Listen to the three people to see if your partner forgot to tell you anything. Whose accent do you prefer? Why?

Grammar

6 Study the yellow phrases in Exercise 4 and complete the Grammar box. Decide if rules 1–4 are T (true) or F (false).

used to		
➕	I _____ walk to school.	
➖	We _____ have much free time.	
❓	Did you _____ enjoy being a lawyer?	

1	Use *used to* for past actions which are now different.	T	F
2	The form of *used to* is the same for all persons.	T	F
3	The negative form is *didn't + used to*.	T	F
4	The question form is *Did + person + used to... ?*	T	F

> AB, p. 104. Ex. 2 ▶

Pronunciation

7 (4.14) Listen to a short dialogue and circle the right answer. Listen again and repeat.

1 How do we pronounce the *s* in *used to*? /s/ or /z/?

2 Do we pronounce the final *d* in *used to*? yes / no

3 How do we pronounce the *to* in *used to*? /tu:/ or /tə/?

Speaking

8 Look back at Exercise 2. Write three sentences about the city using *used to / didn't use to*. Swap with a partner. How many sentences are the same?

There didn't use to be much pollution.

9 In pairs, write sentences comparing your life ten years ago and your life today. Use these ideas or your own.

> clothes education friends
> hobbies home job

A: read your sentences.
B: ask more questions.
Then swap roles.

A: *Ten years ago, I used to live in a big house with my parents and three sisters but now I live in a small flat with a cat!*

B: *Really? / What's its name?*

10 Tell the class something interesting you learned about your partner.

Keeping a record

Pronunciation

1 (4.15) In pairs, how many vowel sounds can you remember? Listen to and look at the 24 vowel pictures in Word Bank 12, p. 75. What are the sounds in each word?

Writing

2 In groups, have a 'chat' online. Use strips of paper as your 'computer'. For five minutes, write as many short questions as you can to everybody in your group and 'send' them to each other to answer. Don't stop writing except to read a question or give back your answers! Who can ask and answer the most questions?

> *Nice shoes. Where did you get them?*

> *R U OK? You look a bit tired.*

> *Have you seen your new boyfriend recently?*

> *Are you working tonight?*

> *Did you watch the game last night?*

3 Swap groups. Compare what you wrote about and answer 1–4. Any surprises?

    1 How often do you 'chat' online or text?

    2 Do you prefer texting, chatting, keying or writing by hand?

    3 Think back to how you used to communicate a few years ago. Is it very different?

    4 Do you think the way we write will change a lot in the future?

Grammar

4 (4.16) Study the grammar box. Then put *back* once in the correct place in each sentence. Listen and check.

> **Verb + *back***
>
> Look **back** through your book.
> Do you usually text **back** immediately?
> Think **back** to how you used to communicate.
>
> ← *Back* is the opposite of *forward* and means *in the opposite direction* or *again*.

> AB, p. 105. Ex. 2 ▶

>   *back*
> Our journey ⁄ after Glastonbury festival last year was horrible. We had to walk to the car in the rain, carrying all our things. But our car didn't start so we left it and took a train to London. Then we had to get a taxi home. We didn't get until 8.30 the next morning. But we're definitely going next year – it was absolutely great!

5 In pairs, look back at Word Bank 2, p. 65. Which of the *get* phrases do we often use with *back*?

Listening

6 Match five of the words and photos, A–E. Have you ever kept records in these ways? Why / Why not? Do you know anybody who does?

> album   blog   diary   letter   mobile phone
> podcast   postcard   videocam   webpage

I used to keep a diary when I was 11, because it was good to write down how I felt.

7 (4.17) Listen to five podcasts about keeping records. Match to photos, A–E.

Pronunciation

8 Turn to page 110. Listen and shadow read. Make the links and pronounce the pink letters /z/ and the blue ones /s/. Is the most common pronunciation for s endings /s/ or /z/?

> **Tip**
> The sound /z/ is voiced.   The sound /s/ is unvoiced.

Reading

9 Quickly read the article from the website. Which of these questions does it answer?

1 Why should we keep a diary?

2 Is it better to keep a paper diary or an electronic one?

3 Who are the three famous diarists?

4 What can we learn about their private lives?

5 Why was it difficult to understand some people's diaries?

Keeping a diary?

Experts say that keeping a diary is good (1) _____ us. When we're angry or worried it helps to write things (2) _____. It's also fascinating to look (3) _____ through our diaries and read about what we used (4) _____ do. Plus it helps us remember details we would otherwise forget too!

Diaries provide a great record (5) _____ future generations too. Famous diarists include Anne Frank and Samuel Pepys who wrote (6) _____ London between 1660 and 1669. It's perhaps the best record of important historical events like the Great Fire of London. But he wrote (7) _____ a special code to stop people reading them! So too did Leonardo Da Vinci.

(A) Perhaps diaries should always stay secret?
(B) Why do people keep them and who are they writing (8) _____? (C) Would you like anybody (9) _____ read your diary before you die?
(D) Do you think it's ever OK (10) _____ read somebody else's diary? Log (11) _____ at magsonline.com and leave your comments.

10 In pairs, choose the correct preposition, 1–11, to complete the text. Then, answer questions A–D in the last paragraph.

1	for / at	7	in / about
2	down / in	8	to / down
3	back / forward	9	into / to
4	up / to	10	for / to
5	for / or	11	on / onto
6	about / through		

Go to **Phrasebook 4** p. 78 ▶   Go to **Essential Grammar 4** p. 118 ▶

1 Correct the sentences. There's one correct sentence.

1 When are you going to finish ~~read~~ *reading* the newspaper?

2 I'm not feel like going out tonight.

3 Swimming is good for you.

4 Our teacher suggested to study together.

5 You're not good in playing musical instruments, are you?

6 The best thing about be a student is meeting people.

7 Do you remember to get lost when we were in Holland?

2 Complete with your own answers.

1 When I'm at home, I enjoy _____ .

2 Personally, I don't mind _____ .

3 I'm really bad at _____ .

4 I'm really interested in _____ .

5 I'm worried about _____ at the moment.

6 _____ is the best way of spending a weekend.

7 _____ is really boring.

8 I gave up _____ because _____ .

3 In pairs, compare your answers to Exercise 2 and give more information.

4 In pairs, look at Phrasebook Units 1–4. How many phrases can you remember? Choose the ten most useful phrases. Then cover and test.

4B 5 (4.18) Listen once. How much did you understand:

25% or less? 50% or less? 75% or less? over 75%?

Tell a partner what you remember.

6 Write T (true) or F (false). Listen and check.

1 Al's brother likes living in Poland. ____

2 People usually do the exchange for half a year. ____

3 Al's brother rents a house. ____

4 Finding a new place to live will be difficult. ____

5 Sara is taking exams at the moment. ____

6 Al will definitely visit his brother. ____

4C 7 In pairs, make sentences. Which pair can make the most, the longest and the funniest sentences in three minutes?

If...

	buy	cold	I'll	do the homework.
it	don't have	me a ticket	I won't	get the DVD.
they	don't like	musicals	we'll	go to the concert.
we	get	some cheese	we won't	make some lunch.
you	go	time	they'll	need sun cream.
	is	to the beach	they won't	put it on the pizza.
				swim in the sea.
				stay indoors.

4D **8** (4.19) Listen and circle the correct option.

1 *Clare / Beppe* pays for breakfast.

2 They meet once a week to *practise languages / have a chat.*

3 Clare *speaks Italian well / has a sexy accent.*

4 Beppe's doing his *first / second* job in computing.

5 A lot of Clare's friends *hate their work / don't have jobs.*

6 Beppe is working for a *business / university.*

7 He *hasn't made any friends yet / has some friends already.*

9 Listen again and complete.

1 **Beppe:** I r_ _ _ _ _ _ need _ _ improve _ _ English.

   Clare: W_ _ _, I think _ _ _ _ English is a _ _ _ better _ _ _ _ my Italian.

2 **Clare:** Well, so _ _ _'s your j_ _ going? Are you enjoying _ _?

   Beppe: Yes, but it's _ lot h_ _ _ _ _ than my _ _ _ _ one.

3 **Beppe:** I earn _ _ _ _ more m_ _ _ _ too, although I _ _ working all _ _ _ time.

   Clare: Really? Well, _ _ _ _ _'s great. _ _ _ _ _ _ days, you're _ _ _ _ _ _ to have _ job.

4 **Beppe:** At l_ _ _ _ my workmates _ _ _ a lot _ _ _ _ _ _ than _ _ my last job.

   Clare: That's _ _ important. So, you're m_ _ _ _ _ some Scottish f_ _ _ _ _ _?

10 Play LANGUAGE EXCHANGE! Get cards from your teacher.

4E **11** In pairs, make five questions about when you were a child with *used to.* Ask and answer. Any big differences?

> what / wear to school?

> look / different?

> how / get to school?

> **When you were ten ...?**

> where / go / in summer?

> what / hobbies / have?

> which / TV programmes / watch?

A: *Did you use to look very different?*

B: *Yes, my hair used to be really long and now it's short and red!*

> **Go to Writing 4 p. 63 ▶**

4F **12** Ask the class, then report your results.

> **Habits questionnaire**
>
> **1** How often do you look back at old ...?
> emails   photos and videos   text messages
> Which do you enjoy most?
>
> **2** How often do you go back to the same place for a holiday?
>
> **3** How many times do you usually go back home on the same day?
>
> **4** Have you ever taken something back to a shop?
>
> **5** Have you ever sent any food back in a restaurant?

13 Play WHAT'S THAT SOUND? Get cards from your teacher. Match three words to each sound. The first pair to match all is the winner.

14 Complete with the verbs. Then answer the final question.

> *sack* (v) = fire (US) to tell someone to leave a job

Teenager sacked for complaining on Facebook!

When 16-year-old Tracey Marshall got a new office job, she wasn't expecting to be in the news. But she was when she was sacked! Like a lot of workers, Tracey spent her time (1) _doing_ (*do*) unimportant tasks. She hated (2) _____ (*use*) the scanner and sorting out documents. So she went on Facebook and started (3) _____ (*put*) her opinions on the site. The comments about being bored were funny for her friends, but she forgot (4) _____ (*stop*) other people looking at the page. Her boss was able (5) _____ (*read*) the comments! He decided (6) _____ (*sack*) Tracey and she had (7) _____ (*leave*) the company. The question in the newspapers was: "Should a boss read workers' comments online?"

> **Song: *Imagine* by John Lennon**
>
> To find the words, google lyric + the name of the song.
>
> To find the video, google video + the name of the song and singer.

9/11

A

September 11th, 2001 was a normal, sunny Tuesday morning in New York. It was nearly 9 a.m. and everybody was going to work as usual when their lives changed forever.

B

But it didn't end there. First, the North Tower and then the South Tower fell and collapsed into downtown New York. It was impossible to believe it was really happening.

C

At the same time, a third plane crashed into the Pentagon. And, finally, a fourth plane crashed in Pennsylvania when the passengers stopped terrorists from flying it into the White House. Altogether, almost three thousand people died on that horrible day.

D

Suddenly a plane crashed into the North Tower of the World Trade Centre. At first everybody thought it was a terrible accident. But while firefighters were trying to stop the fire, another plane hit the South Tower. Everybody tried to help workers at the World Trade Centre to escape, while millions around the world were watching live on TV.

1 Read and order A–D to match headings, 1–4.

1 The scene [ ]   3 And after that? [ ]

2 What happened? [ ]   4 To conclude [ ]

2 Find words in the text with these meanings.

_____ (adv) quickly, without warning

_____ (conj) at the same time as

_____ (v) two objects hit each other fast

_____ (v) to fall suddenly

_____ (conj) at the beginning

_____ (adv) nearly

3 Study the blue words in the text and Writing tip 1. Connect the sentences with *while* or *when* and put the verbs in the correct tense.

1 Emperor Nero ___*played*___ the violin ___*while*___ fires ___*were destroying*___ Rome. (*play, destroy*)

2 _____ the Titanic _____ to New York in 1912, it _____ an iceberg and 1522 people didn't return. (*sail, hit*)

3 _____ doctors _____ to save Michael Jackson, hundreds of fans _____ outside the hospital. (*try, sing*)

4 _____ the 2004 Indian Ocean tsunami _____ Southeast Asia, it _____ over 300,000 people. (*hit, kill*)

Writing tip

1 Use *while* + the Past continuous to describe scenes (*what was happening*).
Use *when* + the Past simple to describe events (*what happened*).

2 Keep sentences simple and interesting with connectors, like the yellow phrases.

4 Write a short story for 'Miracle on the Hudson'.

- Look at the photos and the story prompts.
- Write a draft using headings 1–4 in Exercise 1.
- Include *while*, *when* and the yellow connectors.
- Check articles and tenses carefully.
- Swap drafts with a partner to read and check.
- Finally, give it to your teacher.

January 15th, 2009 / cold, sunny day / New York / plane / take off / LaGuardia Airport.

/ plane / fly / over Manhattan / hit / birds / explosion / fire start.

/ pilot / want / return / LaGuardia. But / no time. So / decide / land / Hudson River.

All 155 passengers / stand / wings and / wait / boats / come.

Vicky Cristina Barcelona

1 I've heard a lot about Woody Allen and I know he's directed over 40 movies. However, it wasn't until last weekend that I saw one of his films when I went to see *Vicky Cristina Barcelona* with my friend.

2 It tells the story of two young American women who travel to Barcelona for their summer holiday. Vicky (Rebecca Hall) is very sensible and engaged. Cristina (Scarlett Johansson) is single and much more adventurous. In Barcelona, they meet Juan Antonio (Javier Bardem), an attractive painter, who has just separated from his crazy ex-wife, Maria Elena (Penélope Cruz).

3 Juan Antonio invites Vicky and Cristina to spend a weekend with him. Although Vicky says she loves her fiancé, she falls in love with Juan. However, Cristina falls in love with him too. But then Maria Elena returns and the love story gets more and more complicated!

4 Although the film didn't cost a lot to make, it's extremely good and the scenery is beautiful too. It's fast and very funny. It's a clever, sexy story about love and life. I really enjoyed it!

posted by Lucy H. at 17.45 p.m.   post a comment

---

1 Read the review to find the names of the characters. Did Lucy like the film?

2 Re-read the review. Which paragraph, 1–4, has this information?

1	the title of the film
☐	the main characters
☐	where they filmed it
☐	what happened next
☐	Lucy's opinions about the film
☐	the beginning of the story
☐	the director
☐	when Lucy watched it and why

3 Read Writing tip 1 and find the ideas being contrasted by the yellow words.

4 Complete sentences 1–4 with *however* or *although*.

1 Vicky says she loves her fiancé. _____, she falls in love with Juan.

2 _____ *Casino Royale*'s one of the best James Bond films, it's not my favourite.

3 Ian Fleming wrote the Bond series in the 1950s. _____, people still love them today.

4 I don't like sci-fi films much _____ I really enjoyed *AI*.

Writing tip

1 Contrast ideas with *although* + clause + comma or *however* + comma.

Although the film didn't cost a lot to make, it's extremely good.

She falls in love with Juan. **However,** Cristina falls in love with him too.

Put *Although* at the start of a sentence which contrasts two things.

Put *However* between two ideas, at the start **or** in the middle of a sentence.

2 Use the Present simple to tell the story of a film or book.

3 Don't repeat adjectives. Think of synonyms or use a dictionary to help you.

5 Read Writing tip 2. Which verb in paragraphs 2 and 3 isn't in the present tense? Is it because it happened

1 very recently and now he's single again?

2 a long time ago so it isn't important now?

6 Read Writing tip 3. Find the opposites of:

cautious	crazy	sad	sensible
simple	stupid	unattractive	

7 Write a review of a film you've seen.

- Write a draft of four paragraphs and include the information from Exercise 2.
- Read it again and check you've followed Writing tips 1–3.
- Swap drafts with a partner to read and check.
- Finally, give it to your teacher.

Welcome to the *Motivating English School* blog!

We all need motivation. So, tell us your learning history and why you are going to learn English with us!

My English learning history

We had to study English at school but I hated it. Lessons were so boring and there were too many kids in our class! We never really spoke.

Since then, I've tried to learn English many times. I've had private classes and been to lots of language schools. But I've always had to stop because of work, life, love, you know, the usual!

Now, I'm 28, a phone engineer, and have to learn English quickly for my job! So I've been on this course for five months. We have lessons twice a week, for two hours, without a break! Our teacher's tough with us! We mustn't speak Portuguese and have to do the homework or she gets angry, which is good. I also practise on my own. Most websites I read are in English and I watch cable TV a lot too.

My listening and writing are getting better but I need to work on my speaking. I'm not going to give up again because I'm taking an exam in January. If I pass, my company will send me to the UK for a year! So, I'm really motivated this time!

What about you?

posted by Jose Pereira, Coimbra, Portugal at 15:32 p.m. on Monday, 5th July

[Post a comment]

1 Read the blog quickly, then cover. What do you remember about Jose's ... ?

age and job   course   future plans   learning history

2 Re-read and check. Number questions A–H in the order he answers them, 1–8.

A Has your English improved since you started the course?

B What else do you do to learn English outside class?

C What's your teacher like and what are your class rules?

D What exactly is your goal in English?

E How long have you been on the course?

F Have you studied English privately before? How and where?

G Did you learn much English at school? Why (not)?   *1*

H How often do you have classes and how long is each one?

Writing tip

Tenses

Ask yourself is / was the action:

● in the past, present or future?

● once only or repeated? Has it finished? Do you know when?

● a habit, an obligation, a plan, a promise?

3 Read the Writing tip. Tick the correct sentences. Correct the wrong ones.

1 I've learned English for six years when I was at school.

2 I studied English in many places before.

3 I've been at this school for over a year.

4 I didn't like my teachers at school.

5 I'm go to classes three times a week.

6 I'll to finish my exams next year.

7 I want to learn English for to travel abroad.

4 Study the yellow words in the blog and match to the correct use.

to   infinitive / direction

in   preposition of *place / time*

for   preposition of *time / purpose*

5 Write your own English learning history for the blog.

● Write a draft of four paragraphs. Answer questions A–H from Exercise 2 in the same order as Jose.

● Read it again and check you've followed the Writing tips.

● Swap drafts with a partner to read and check.

● Finally, give it to your teacher.

Jobsforall

Bilingual speakers wanted to help at the next Olympic Games.

If you are good with people, have at least Intermediate English and would like to spend a month helping visitors to the UK, please e-mail your CV and a covering letter to olympicuk.com. Includes flights, accommodation, help with visa, training and a good salary!

(1) Dear Sir or Madam

I saw your advert on the Jobsforall website and am writing **(2)** to apply for the job of Olympic helper.

I am bilingual in Korean and Spanish as my mother is South Korean and my father is Mexican. I have lived in both countries and have also studied English for three years.

As you will see from my CV, I have worked in a clothes shop, bookshop and restaurant. When I was at university, I also did voluntary work for the disabled, so **(3)** I have a lot of experience with people of different ages and needs.

I am very interested in working for you because I would enjoy being part of the Olympic Games. I really believe in the Olympic idea and like helping people. I am sure it will help me learn a lot about your country's culture and improve my English too.

(4) I attach my CV with two referees. **(5)** Please feel free to contact me if you need more information or call me at any time for an interview.

(6) I look forward to hearing from you.

(7) Yours sincerely,
Kim Lee Jung

---

1 Read the advert and find

  1 three qualifications needed for the job.

  2 two things applicants need to send.

  3 five advantages of the job.

2 Read the e-mail to find out

  1 if Kim has the three qualifications.

  2 the four jobs he's done.

  3 his reasons for wanting the job.

  4 if he sends the right things.

Do you think Kim is a good candidate?

Writing tip

  1 In formal e-mails, use expressions like the ones in yellow.

  2 Separate your ideas into clear, short paragraphs.

  3 Don't use contractions, lots of exclamation marks (!!!), abbreviations (except CV) or text speak.

3 Read Writing tip 1. Match the expressions in yellow to their informal equivalents.

  1 C U soon

  2 Because I want

  3 Hello / Hi!

  4 love from

  5 **Pls call me**

  6 *I'm sending my history with two friends' names.*

  7 *I know what I'm doing!!!*

4 Write an e-mail to apply for the job.

- Divide your e-mail into the same paragraphs as Kim.
- Include your qualifications, jobs and reasons for wanting the job.
- Read it again and check you've followed Writing tips 1–3.
- Swap drafts with a partner to read and check.
- Finally, give it to your teacher.

1 (1.1) Match the adjectives and pictures, 1–10. Listen and check. What's the weather like?

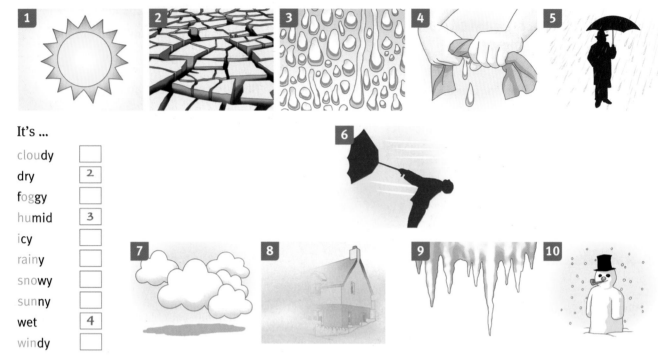

It's ...

cloudy [ ]
dry [2]
foggy [ ]
humid [3]
icy [ ]
rainy [ ]
snowy [ ]
sunny [ ]
wet [4]
windy [ ]

2 Cover the words. Point to a picture and test a partner.

A: *What's the weather like?*   **B:** *It's cloudy. What's ... ?*

3 Match the nouns and pictures, 11–15. Which two are uncountable?
What happened yesterday? Listen and check.

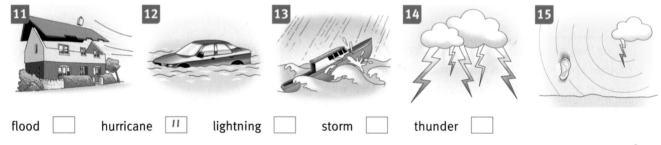

flood [ ]   hurricane [11]   lightning [ ]   storm [ ]   thunder [ ]

4 Match phrases a–d with speech bubbles, 16–19. Listen and check.   ◄ 1A p.4

a It's boiling!
b It's cold.
c It's freezing!
d It's warm.

What's the temperature?

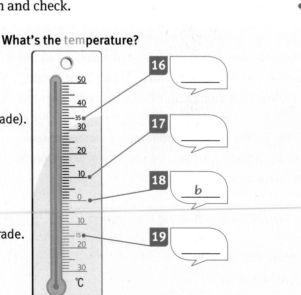

It's about 35 (degrees Centigrade).

It's ten degrees above zero.

It's one degree below zero.

It's minus 15 degrees Centigrade.

16 [ ]
17 [ ]
18 [b]
19 [ ]

The verb *get*

1 (1.8) Match five of the phrases to pictures, 1–5. Listen and check.

get (+ adjective) = become	get = *obtain* or ____	get = ____	get = ____	get = ____
married ☐4	a job ☐	a text ☐	a bus ☐	home ☐
ready ☐	some stamps ☐	____	____	to work / school ☐
____				____

2 Match each group in Exercise 1 to these meanings. Then add another example to each group.

arrive at   ~~become~~   buy   ~~obtain~~   receive   travel by

3 In pairs, ask and answer *When was the last time ... ?* or *How often do you ... ?*

A: *When was the last time you got a text message?*   **B:** *Five minutes ago, from my friend. What about you?*   1C p.8

---

4 (3.7) Match the phrases and pictures, 6–11. Listen and check.

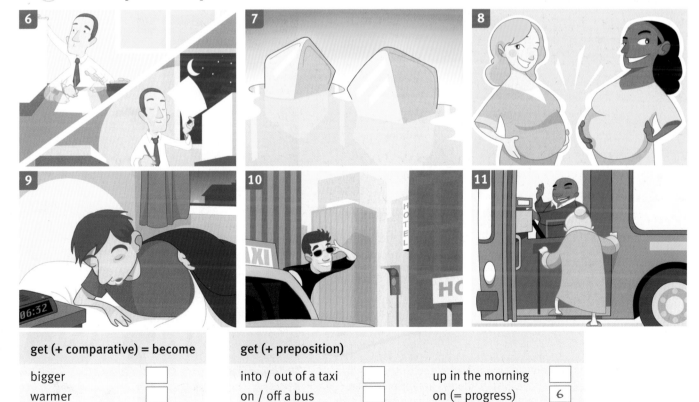

get (+ comparative) = become		get (+ preposition)			
bigger ☐		into / out of a taxi ☐		up in the morning ☐	
warmer ☐		on / off a bus ☐		on (= progress) ☐6	

5 In pairs, make sentences for each phrase.

A + B: *We think the world is getting warmer.*

3C p.36   4F p.56

Travel problems

1 (1.12) Match the problems and pictures, 1–4. Then match the other problems and pictures, 5–10. Listen and check.

get lost ☐   get stuck in traffic ☐ 4   get travel sick ☐   get wet ☐

flight delayed / cancelled ☐   leave something on the train ☐   miss the bus ☐
forget your passport ☐   lose your ticket ☐ 6   have to wait in a long queue / line ☐

2 Test a partner. Point to a picture and ask what happened.

A: *What happened to him?*   **B:** *His flight was delayed. What happened to them?*   1D p.10

American and British English

1 (1.15) Match the pairs of words to pictures, 1–10. Listen and check.

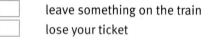 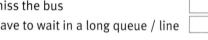

	🇺🇸	🇬🇧
6 buy some	candy	sweets
☐ eat a	cookie	biscuit
☐ get the	subway	underground
☐ go shopping in a	store	shop
☐ have a	vacation	holiday
☐ play in the	yard	garden
☐ see a	movie	film
☐ take the	elevator	lift
☐ use a	cell (phone)	mobile (phone)
5 walk	downtown	to the town centre
	I have (a car).	*I've got (a car).*

2 Test a partner. A: Give the American word.
B: Say the British one. Swap roles.

A: *the subway*   **B:** *the underground*   1E p.12

Tip

There are some small differences in American and British English vocabulary like the ones above. Some sounds are different, especially the letters *r* and *o*, and the Americans also say /ziː/ for the letter *z* /zed/.

British English usually uses *have got*, but American English uses *have*, and this is more common internationally.

Going on holiday

1 (1.17) Match the activities and pictures, 1–12. Listen and check. Think of another verb for each pattern.

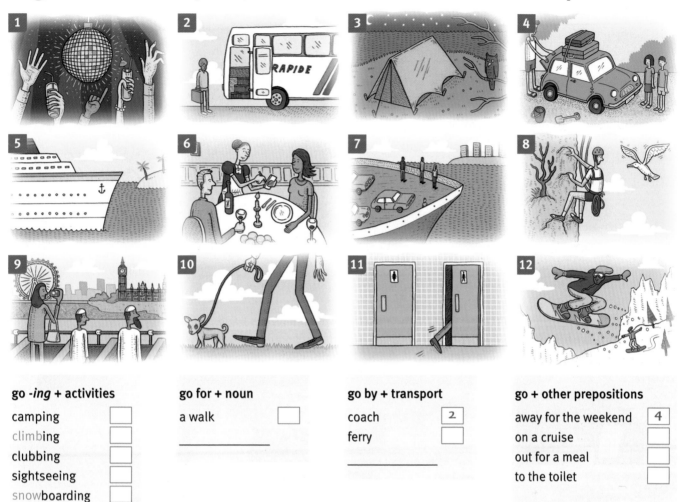

go -*ing* + activities

camping	
climbing	
clubbing	
sightseeing	
snowboarding	

_____

go for + noun

a walk	

_____

go by + transport

coach	2
ferry	

_____

go + other prepositions

away for the weekend	4
on a cruise	
out for a meal	
to the toilet	

_____

2 Match activities and pictures, 13–20. Listen and check.

buy souvenirs		hire a car		rent an apartment	14	try new food	
have a good time / fun		meet new people		sunbathe		visit museums	

3 Which of the activities on this page do you usually do on holiday? In pairs, compare answers.

1F p.14

1 (2.1) Match the adjectives and pictures, 1–8. Pronounce them with the correct stress. Which two are opposites? Listen and check.

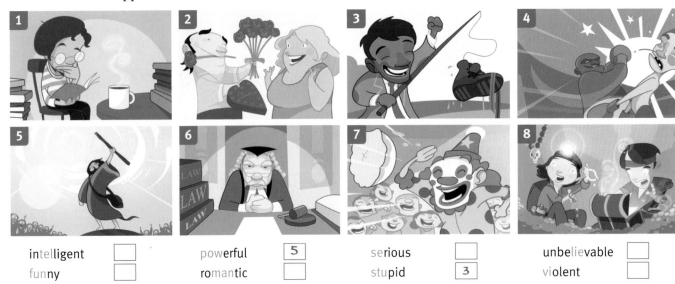

inte**lli**gent	☐	**pow**erful	5	**se**rious	☐	unbe**lie**vable	☐
funny	☐	ro**man**tic	☐	**stu**pid	3	**vi**olent	☐

2 Match the adjectives and pictures, 9–16. Which two are opposites? Which two are negative? Listen and check.

a**ma**zing	☐	con**fu**sing	☐	ex**ci**ting	13	re**la**xing	☐
boring	☐	disa**ppoin**ting	☐	**in**teresting	☐	**sca**ry	14

3 Cover the words. Look at the pictures. In pairs, practise saying the words together. 2A p.18

Personality adjectives

4 (2.7) Match and circle one adjective in each pair to pictures, 17–22. Listen, check and repeat the pairs.

calm /(e**ner**getic)	18	**friend**ly / un**friend**ly	☐	po**lite** / **rude**	21
extrovert / **shy**	☐	**gen**tle / a**ggre**ssive	☐	**tal**kative / **qui**et	☐

5 Cover the page. In pairs, remember as many adjectives as you can.  2C p.22 4D p.52

1 (2.10) Match the words with the computer equipment, 1–9. Stress the words correctly. Listen and check.

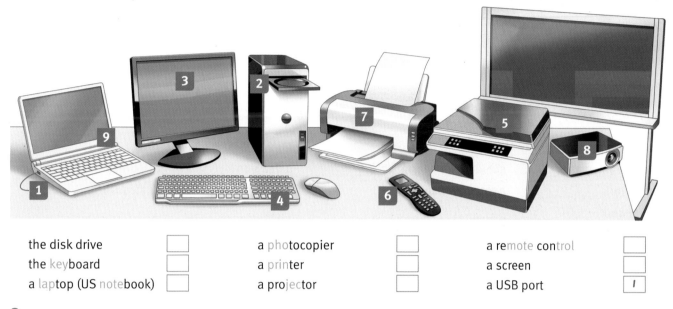

the disk drive ☐	a photocopier ☐	a remote control ☐
the keyboard ☐	a printer ☐	a screen ☐
a laptop (US notebook) ☐	a projector ☐	a USB port `1`

2 Match these verbs and phrases, a–o. Then match eight to pictures, 10–17. Listen and check.

~~attach~~	charge	chat	click	create	delete	download	go
~~have~~	install	key	make	start	type	upgrade	

    a   a_ttach_____ (a file)

    b   c_____ a new spreadsheet

`11` **c**   _start_____ up (the computer)

☐ **d**   g_____ online = connect to the Internet

☐ **e**   ch_____ (on MSN)

    f   _____ a blog / photolog

☐ **g**   c_____ on (a link)

    h   _____ in (your password)

`14` **i**   _have_____ a WiFi connection

☐ **j**   _____ fast

☐ **k**   d_____ (spam)

    l   _____ (your computer)

☐ **m**   c_____ (a phone)

☐ **n**   d_____ (a file)

    o   _____ software

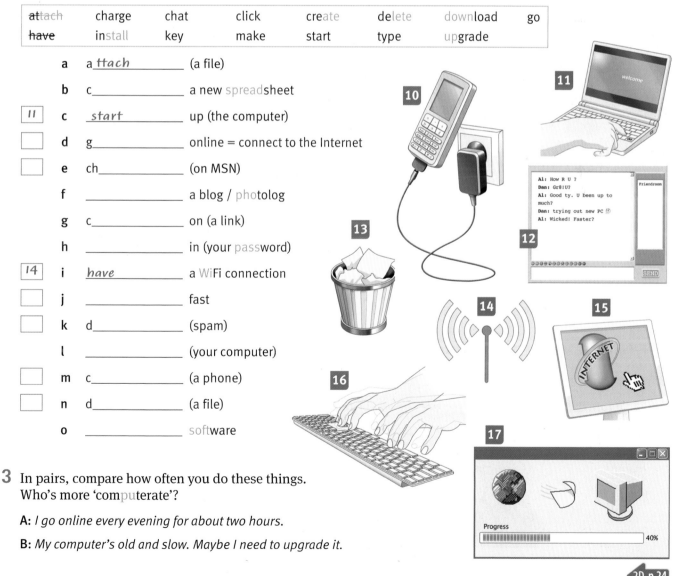

3 In pairs, compare how often you do these things. Who's more 'computerate'?

A: *I go online every evening for about two hours.*

B: *My computer's old and slow. Maybe I need to upgrade it.*

2D p.24

1 (2.19) Match five of the *do* and *make* phrases to pictures, 1–5. Listen and check. Add three more phrases.

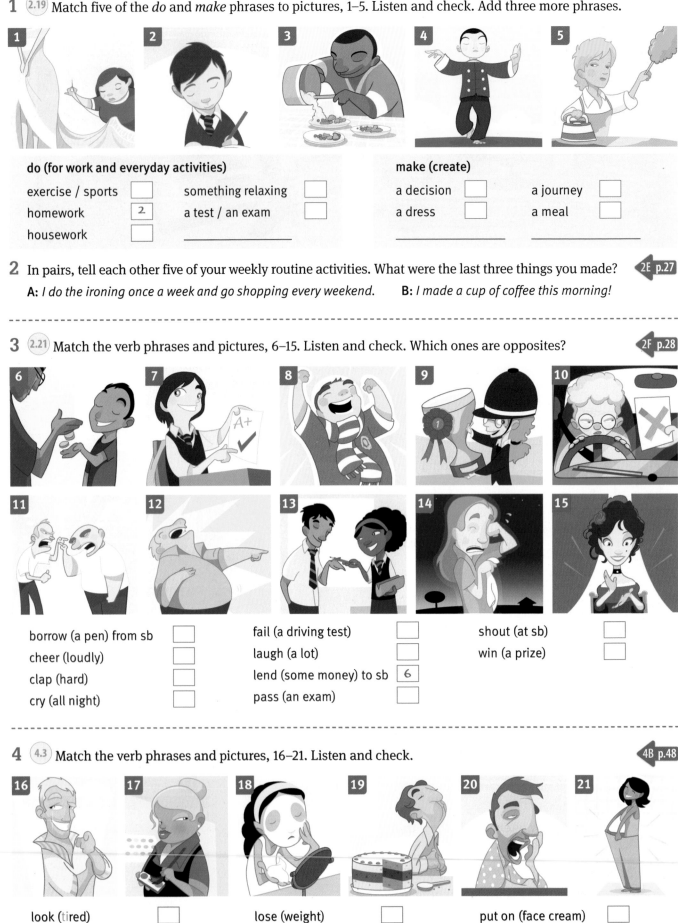

do (for work and everyday activities)

exercise / sports ☐	something relaxing ☐
homework 2	a test / an exam ☐
housework ☐	_____

make (create)

a decision ☐	a journey ☐
a dress ☐	a meal ☐
_____	_____

2 In pairs, tell each other five of your weekly routine activities. What were the last three things you made?   2E p.27

A: *I do the ironing once a week and go shopping every weekend.*   **B:** *I made a cup of coffee this morning!*

3 (2.21) Match the verb phrases and pictures, 6–15. Listen and check. Which ones are opposites?   2F p.28

borrow (a pen) from sb ☐	fail (a driving test) ☐	shout (at sb) ☐
cheer (loudly) ☐	laugh (a lot) ☐	win (a prize) ☐
clap (hard) ☐	lend (some money) to sb 6	
cry (all night) ☐	pass (an exam) ☐	

4 (4.3) Match the verb phrases and pictures, 16–21. Listen and check.   4B p.48

look (tired) ☐	lose (weight) ☐	put on (face cream) ☐
look like (a model) 16	regret (eating a cake) ☐	wear (make up) ☐

Verbs, adjectives and prepositions

1 (3.1) Match a–j with pictures, 1–10. Complete the opposites of a–f. Listen and check.

	Verb and preposition	Opposite
a	**2** come in	go _out_
b	☐ log on	log _____
c	☐ pick up (a pen)	put _____
d	☐ put on (headphones)	take _____
e	☐ sit down	stand _____
f	☐ turn on (a printer)	turn _____
g	☐ fill in (a form)	
h	☐ look up (a word in a dictionary)	
i	☐ print out (some pages)	
j	**9** write down (some words)	

2 Test your partner.
A: Mime the action. B: Say what A's doing.
Swap roles.

3 Say when you do these actions and why.

A: *I write down words when I'm in class, because I want to remember them.*

3A p.32

---

4 Match the adjectives and pictures, 1–8.

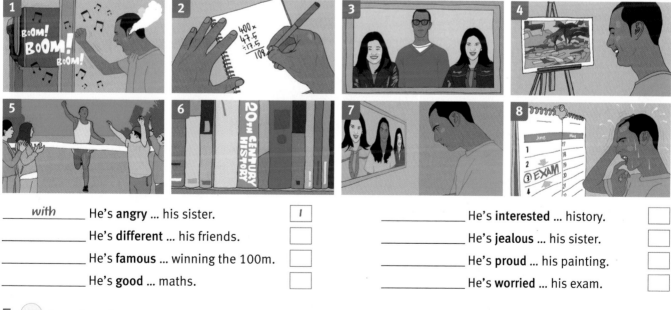

___*with*___ He's **angry** ... his sister.	**1**	_____ He's **interested** ... history.	☐
_____ He's **different** ... his friends.	☐	_____ He's **jealous** ... his sister.	☐
_____ He's **famous** ... winning the 100m.	☐	_____ He's **proud** ... his painting.	☐
_____ He's **good** ... maths.	☐	_____ He's **worried** ... his exam.	☐

5 (4.1) Complete the sentences in Exercise 4 with the missing preposition. Listen and check.

about   at   for   from   in   of (× 2)   ~~with~~

6 Cover the prepositions and test yourself. Can you remember them all?

4A p.46

1 (3.11) Match the words to the places on the map, 1–9. Listen and check. 3D p.38

a bridge ☐	a pedestrian crossing (US crosswalk) ☐	a roundabout ☐
an exit (from a motorway) `3`	a road sign ☐	traffic lights (US lights) ☐
a motorway (US highway) ☐	roadworks (US road work) ☐	a tunnel ☐

2 (3.15) Match the directions with pictures, 10–21. Listen and check. Test your partner on directions.

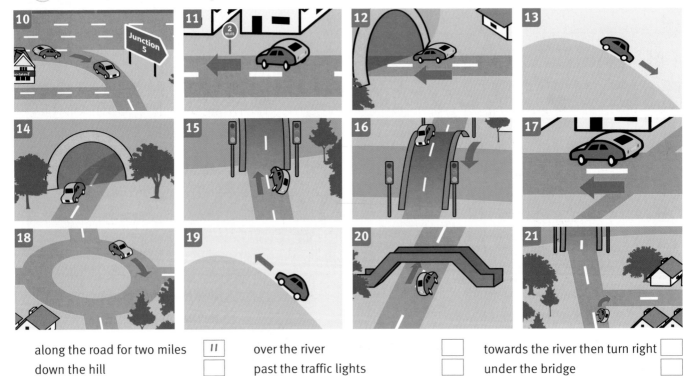

along the road for two miles `11`	over the river ☐	towards the river then turn right ☐
down the hill ☐	past the traffic lights ☐	under the bridge ☐
into the tunnel ☐	round the roundabout ☐	up the hill ☐
out of the tunnel ☐	straight ahead ☐	turn right at the junction ☐

3 Ask your partner to describe his / her journey today. How many phrases from Exercise 2 do they use? 3D p.39

1 (3.18) Match the phrasal verbs and pictures, 1–8. Listen and check.

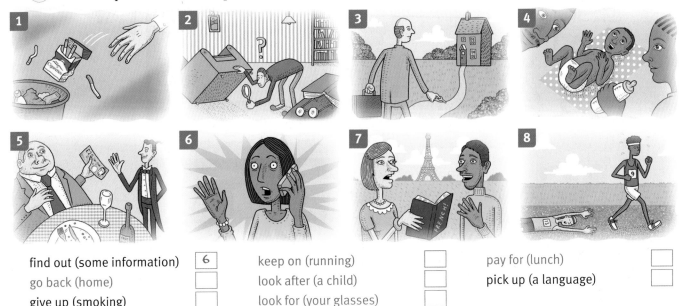

find out (some information)	6	keep on (running)		pay for (lunch)	
go back (home)		look after (a child)		pick up (a language)	
give up (smoking)		look for (your glasses)			

2 Match the phrasal verbs and pictures, 9–20. Listen and check. Test your partner on phrasal verbs.

call back		hurry up		stay up		try on	
come in		look forward (to)	18	take off (your coat)		turn down / up	
grow up		put on (make up)		throw away		wake up	

3 Have you done any of the things in Exercises 1 and 2 recently? What and when?

A: *I've looked after children recently. I looked after my sister's two daughters last Friday.*

B: *I stayed up late on Monday. I was very tired the next day!*

 3F p.43

Rules

Phrasal verbs

no object: verb and preposition do not separate

+ object: verb and preposition do not separate
Look after my baby. NOT *Look* my baby *after*.

+ object: verb and preposition can separate
Turn the volume *up*. OR *Turn up* the volume.

1 Match comments, a–i, to pictures, 1–9.

a _____ *I **asked** ... a black coffee. This is white.*

b _____ *She **asked** him ... carry one of her bags.*

c _____ *I don't **care** ... that. I hate tennis!*

d _____ *We **congratulated** him ... reaching 100.*

e _____ *I've **lost touch** ... all my school friends.*

f _____ *I'm really sorry. I'll **pay** ... the damage.*

g _____ *Most people **prefer** meat ... cheese.*

h _____ *I **spent** all my money ... souvenirs.*

4 i _____ *While you're away, **think** ... me at work!*

j *with* *I really don't **agree** ... you.*

k _____ *I'm going to **apply** ... a new job.*

l _____ *Most people **believe** ... luck.*

m _____ *Ssh! I can't **concentrate** ... the match.*

n _____ *It **depends** ... the weather.*

o _____ *She **explained** the homework ... us.*

p _____ *What **happened** ... the jeans I lent you?*

q _____ *Chris Brown? I've never **heard** ... him!*

r _____ *Can you **help** me ... the homework?*

s _____ *I often **listen** ... podcasts.*

t _____ ***Look** ... that view – it's amazing.*

u _____ *We **searched** ... a cheap hotel.*

v _____ *I **talked** ... the doctor for hours.*

w _____ *Don't **translate** from English ... your language.*

x _____ *I **waited** ... the bus all morning.*

2 (4.8) Write the missing preposition next to each sentence, a–x. Listen and check.

about   at   for (× 5)   in   into   of (× 2)
on (× 4)   to (× 6)   with (× 3)

3 Cover the prepositions and test yourself.   4C p.50

4.15 **20 vowel sounds**   Listen and repeat.

7 short vowels

 ɪ
 æ
 e
 ɒ

 ʌ ¹
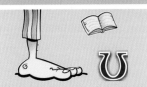 ʊ
 ə

5 long vowels

 iː
 ɑː
 ɜː
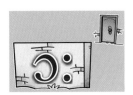 ɔː
 uː

8 diphthongs

 eɪ
 aɪ
 əʊ
 aʊ

 eə
 ɪə
 ɔɪ
ʊə

4F p.56

3.6 **24 consonant sounds**   Listen and repeat the nine red unvoiced and 15 voiced consonants.

 p
 b
 k
 g
 f
v

t
d
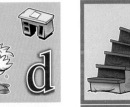 s
z
ʃ
ʒ

θ
ð
 tʃ
dʒ
h
l

r
 w
 j
 m
 n
ŋ

Word Bank 13   Irregular verbs

1 Race to test your partner on the past simple forms in the chart. Which pair can remember them all first?

 1A p.5

Infinitive	Past simple	Past participle
be	was / were	been
become	became	become
buy	bought	bought
come	came	come
do	did	_____
drink	drank	_____
drive	drove	_____
eat	ate	_____
feel	felt	felt
find	found	found
fly	flew	
forget	forgot	
get	got	got
give	gave	
go	went	_____
have	had	had
hear	heard	heard
keep	kept	kept
leave	left	left
make	made	made
meet	met	met
put	put	put
read /ri:d/	read /ri:d/	read /red/
ride	rode	_____
say	said	said
sell	sold	sold
see	saw	_____
send	sent	sent
sing	sang	
sleep	slept	slept
speak	spoke	_____
spend	spent	spent
take	took	taken
teach	taught	taught
tell	told	told
think	thought	thought
understand	understood	understood
wake	woke	_____
win	won	won
write	wrote	_____

2 Complete the chart with these past participles. Why are they in five groups?

done	forgotten	eaten	driven	flown
drunk	gone	seen	ridden	spoken
sung			written	woken

2B p.21

3 **1** Cover the Past simple column and test yourself.
  2 Do the same with the Past participle column.

 R1 p.16

Infinitive	Past simple	Past participle
begin	began	begun
break	broke	broken
bring	brought	brought
build	built	built
can	could	been able to
catch	caught	caught
choose	chose	chosen
cost	cost	cost
cut	cut	cut
fall	fell	fallen
fight	fought	fought
freeze	froze	frozen
grow	grew	grown
hide	hid	hidden
hit	hit	hit
hold	held	held
know	knew	known
learn	learnt	learnt
lend	lent	lent
let	let	let
lose	lost	lost
mean	meant	meant
pay	paid	paid
ring	rang	rung
run	ran	run
set	set	set
shine	shone	shone
show	showed	shown
shut	shut	shut
sit	sat	sat
stand	stood	stood
steal	stole	stolen
stick	stuck	stuck
swim	swam	swum
throw	threw	thrown
wear	wore	worn

4 Look at both charts and answer questions 1–3.
  1 Why are some verbs black, blue or red?
  2 Do most irregular verbs have one or two syllables?
  3 Which past participles rhyme with *ought* and *read*?

 3E p.40

Unit 1

1 (P.1) Listen. Translate the phrases in pencil.

English	Your language
It doesn't matter.	
How was your holiday?	
We had a wonderful time.	
I'm really into ...	
Why didn't you tell me?	
No, not at all.	
There wasn't time.	
Nobody wanted to go.	
For example, ...	
Don't miss it!	
Maybe twice a week.	
Is everything OK?	
Wow! That's good!	
Thanks a million.	
How exciting!	
It's going to be brilliant!	
It's open all night.	
Don't forget to write.	
For work or pleasure?	
Go away!	
I'll meet you outside.	
Where were you going?	
I couldn't believe it!	
They were all cancelled!	
It was still raining.	
It's good / bad for you.	
What a good idea!	

2 Test yourself regularly. Cover one column and remember the other.

Unit 2

1 Erase the translations in Unit 1 you don't need now.

2 (P.2) Listen. How do you say these phrases in your language? Translate the phrases in pencil.

English	Your language
I really enjoyed it.	
Pass the sugar.	
Since then ...	
all over the world	
If you're under 18.	
She's gorgeous!	
Not bad I suppose.	
He's quite intelligent.	
A bit boring.	
He's famous for ...	
all the time	
He's always complaining.	
I mean ...	
In fact, ...	
I bet it rains.	
a few days	
Unfortunately ...	
Oh dear.	
To be honest ...	
I'm so glad.	
I'm starving!	
It was worth it.	
I felt sorry for her.	
Apart from that ...	
What's up?	
It's such a beautiful area.	
Anyway, ...	

3 Listen to your CD regularly and translate the phrases in Units 1 and 2 in your mind.

Phrasebook

Unit 3

1 Erase the translations in Units 1 and 2 you don't need now.

2 (P.3) Listen and translate the phrases in pencil.

English	Your language
by 2050	
about fifty-fifty	
How does it work?	
Not during the lesson.	
How long have you been here?	
Wow, time flies!	
Lucky you!	
I adore Mexico!	
It's fun!	
That was very noisy!	
We both speak quite well.	
I see ...	
He's the guy who ...	
Any more questions?	
Come on – try me!	
I know what you mean.	
Do you give up?	
I've never heard of that!	
I didn't know either.	
In my opinion, ...	
Not far.	
Could you give me a clue?	
That was ages ago!	
But that's impossible.	
Who knows?	
Have a great trip!	

3 Test yourself until you can remember them all.

Unit 4

1 Test yourself on Units 1, 2 and 3. Erase the translations you don't need now.

2 (P.4) Listen and translate the phrases in pencil.

English	Your language
I was so worried about ...	
I felt like crying.	
I'll never forget it.	
It's time to go.	
So what are you waiting for?	
Go on – try it!	
It might be.	
It might not.	
You won't regret it!	
Have you seen this?	
Not yet.	
That's not true.	
I agree with that.	
Only joking.	
I haven't finished.	
I'm enjoying this.	
I don't earn enough!	
It's really unfair.	
That's not fair.	
a friend of mine	
And what's more ...	
exactly the same	
I certainly hope so.	
I decided to give it up.	
I work as a nurse.	
To tell the truth ...	
I prefer dogs to cats.	

3 Try to remember all the phrases in this Phrasebook!

What was the weather like?

Vocabulary

Word Bank 1: The weather p. 64   **Word Bank 13:** Irregular verbs p. 76
Nouns: firefighter, forest fire, headlines, news, rescue team, seasons, tour
Adjectives: awful, brave, empty-handed, expensive, memorable, similar
Verbs: check, disappear, happen, invite, refuse, remember, stay
Adverbs: exactly, quite, really   **Other:** somebody, something, sometime
Expressions: It didn't matter. I'm not sure. It's cool. Let's go!

1 Order the words to complete the weather reports.

1 There are two major weather problems this morning. There are very strong (1) _____winds_____ (dinws) in the southern USA because of the (2) _____ (nuharcier) in the Caribbean. It's raining very hard and there are (3) _____ (doslof) in many Florida cities. In California, the forest fires are continuing and many homes are in (4) _____ (nadreg). The problem is the hot weather: it's still 38 (5) _____ (sedeerg) in San Diego and 35 in LA.

2 There isn't any (6) _____ (uns) in the UK today. It'll be (7) _____ (cyodlu) all over the country. There are also (8) _____ (gezrefin) temperatures in the North: -4 in Manchester and Liverpool. Finally, driving will be (9) _____ (rudnagose) in Scotland because of the (10) _____ (troms) last night.

2 **(1.1)** Listen. Circle T (true) or F (false).

1 It's raining today.   T / F
2 They decide to go to Sitges.   T / F
3 Sitges is a good place for shopping.   T / F

3 Match the questions to the answers.

1 What are your parents like?
2 What's your flat like?
3 What was that film like last night?
4 What were the desserts like at that café?
5 What was your last teacher like?
6 What were your English lessons like at school?

a ☐ Really boring. We never spoke, just wrote sentences and studied grammar.

b ☐ My father's dead, sadly. My mum's very friendly. She really loves people.

c ☐ Great. We really enjoyed it. Brilliant acting. But a bit long.

d ☐ It's modern, quite small but very light. Just one bedroom.

e ☐ She wasn't bad. But sometimes I didn't understand her very well.

f ☐ Nothing special. The chocolate cake was nice, but the rest were only OK.

4 Correct the questions.

1 ~~You do not~~ *Don't you* speak English?
2 *Is good the weather in your country?*
3 **What means 'package holiday'?**
4 *Why didn't tell you me before?*
5 *What time started the lesson?*
6 *Isn't you the new teacher?*
7 *With who did you go to the party?*

5 Paula's a student at a language school in London. She writes an e-mail to her teacher, Martin. Find and circle six more mistakes in the email.

Hi Martin

My name's Paula da Sousa and I'm ~~I~~ from Brazil. I live with my mother and my sister Carolina in Rio de Janeiro. Carolina has 16 and she's still in school. I also have a brother but he don't live with us. He's 25 years and he live in São Paolo. He's engineer. He get married a year ago and last month they have a beautiful baby boy.

I'm a student in the moment but I want to work as doctor. I'm study Medicine at university and I'm finally going finish my course on June next year.

In my free time, I play tennis and basketball. I also like read books in English.

Paula

Saving the planet

Vocabulary

Nouns: academy, activity, amount, building, business, chimney, climate, danger, documentary, environment, expert, factory, ferry, global warming, issues, metal, plastic, polluter, pollution, poster, prize, recycling, speaker, trailer, tram, truth, underwear

Adjectives: award-winning, enormous, former, inconvenient, natural, powerful, scary, scientific

Verbs: believe, carry, collect, destroy, include, miss, organise, pollute, present, recycle, reduce, ride

Adverbs: actually, fully, never, normally, often, still, usually

Expressions: Is it good? That's terrible. Let's hope so.

1 Complete the comments. There's one extra word.

> destroy   documentary   experts   factories
> former   ice   pollutes   warming

Zara: *"If we don't stop climate change, it will _____ the environment."*

Chen: *"I saw a really frightening _____ on TV about the problems in the rain forests. It was awful."*

Dieter: *"The _____ say that the country needs to use less petrol".*

Xavier: *"Most of the chemicals in the rivers comes from local _____ ."*

Louise: *"Governments still put rubbish in the sea. It _____ the water and it kills fish and other animals."*

Seija: *"The film showed a photo of a polar bear alone on the _____ . It made me feel really sad."*

Marco: *"Global _____ is making the planet hotter. We have to stop it!"*

2 Order the sentences and add one preposition.

1 you / travel / often / how / plane / do ?

_____

2 work / walk / never / I

_____

3 sometimes / Owen / rides / his / school / bike

_____

4 tram / a / travel / we / twice / week

_____

5 the / Li / train / breakfast / has / always

_____

3 Circle the correct option.

Harry: Hi Paula. What (1) *are you watching / do you watch*?

Paula: It's a documentary about tigers with Kurt Gerlach.

Harry: Oh. (2) *I'm really liking / I really like* his programmes. Is it good?

Paula: Yeah, but it's really frightening. (3) *Are you knowing / Do you know* that there are only 500 Siberian tigers left in the wild?

Harry: That's terrible. What (4) *does Gerlach think / is Gerlach thinking* about it?

Paula: (5)*He is believing / He believes* we can still save the tiger. Watch the programme with me!

Harry: I can't. (6) *I go / I'm going* out.

4 Correct the sentences. There's one correct sentence.

1 ☐ I'm not working very hard at the moment.

2 ☐ I'm having two brothers.

3 ☐ We're usually driving to school.

4 ☐ Are you knowing the Palace Theatre?

5 ☐ We're watching *An Inconvenient Truth* tonight.

5 (1.2) Listen and circle the correct option.

1 Where's Pete? *In a car. / On a train.*

2 Pete usually travels by *car / plane / train.*

3 To get to Glasgow takes *five / nine* hours.

4 Pete's reading a *book / newspaper.*

5 Pete prefers the *plane / train.*

6 In Glasgow it's *raining / snowing.*

6 Listen again and try the Study tip.

Study tip

1 Use your student CD to practise pronunciation. When you finish a listening exercise, listen again to the recording. Stop the CD after sentences which you find interesting, unusual or difficult and repeat. Try to sound like the speakers.

2 Or, for fun, pause the recording in the middle of a sentence. Try to complete the sentence then listen and check if you were right.

I'm going to relax by the pool

Vocabulary

Word Bank 2: The verb *get* p. 65

Nouns: beef, casino, channel, coat, dessert, guidebook, link, lunchtime, machine, main course, mini bar, operator, plaster, salad, seafood, sightseeing, steak, trip

Adjectives: medium, non-alcoholic, rare, Swiss, well-done

Verbs: arrange, feel, sunbathe, surf   **Adverbs:** actually, certainly, just, nearly

Expressions: Nothing for me thanks. Not quite. Do you want to come? Thanks for inviting me.

1 Complete the puzzle. What's the word in grey?

1 I need some money. Is there a _____ machine in the hotel?

2 There is a local _____ operator who arranges sightseeing trips to the mountains.

3 We have all the main TV channels but if you want to watch a movie, the rooms also have _____ TV.

4 There are drinks in your hotel room in the _____ bar.

5 If you feel hot, turn on the air- _____ .

6 You can surf the web in your hotel room, because we have internet _____ .

7 My girlfriend wants to go to the _____ salon .

8 If you want dinner in your hotel room, ask for room _____ .

2 Match the questions to the answers.

1 Good evening. Are you ready to order?

2 I'll have the salad to start and then the steak.

3 How about dessert?

4 May we have the bill?

a ☐ Nothing for me, thanks.

b ☐ Would you like it rare, medium, or well-done?

c ☐ Certainly. I'll get it for you now.

d ☐ Not quite. Can we have another minute, please?

3 Read the situations and complete the sentences.

1 The waiter asks "Would you like chicken, salmon or beef for your main course?"

You say: I think I _____ have _____ salmon.

2 You're eating with a friend in a restaurant. The bill arrives and you decide to invite him.

You say: Don't worry. I _____ pay _____ it!

3 Your friend's cooking but doesn't have any salt.

You say: I _____ go _____ the shop and get some _____ you if you like?

4 A friend is outside your house, looking a bit tired.

You say: Come in. I _____ make you _____ nice cup _____ tea. It _____ take me long.

5 Your friends are leaving your flat. But it's raining.

You say: Don't walk. We _____ take you _____ the station _____ our car.

4 (1.3) Order the dialogue, 1–7. Listen and check.

a ☐ I can't. I haven't got any money.

b ☐ Yeah, it is. It's 12.30.

c ☐ Nearly. I'll just get my coat.

d ☐ Would you like to have lunch in that new café?

e ☐ *1* It's nearly lunchtime.

f ☐ OK. Thanks. Are you ready to go now?

g ☐ That's OK. I'll pay.

5 (1.4) Circle the correct option. Listen and check.

Tino: (1) *I'll go / I'm going to go* on holiday on Friday.

Marta: Really? Where (2) *will you go / are you going to go*?

Tino: The Swiss Alps. (3) *I'll do / I'm going to do* a skiing course for a week in Zermatt.

Marta: Hey, I've got a guidebook of Switzerland. (4) *I'll bring / I'm going to bring* it into work for you tomorrow.

Tino: Thanks! That (5) *'ll / 's going to* be great.

Marta: I also know a good website about the Alps. (6) *I'll send / I'm going to send* you the link this evening.

Tino: Thanks. You know a lot about Switzerland!

Marta: Yeah. My grandma's Swiss. Actually, me and my brother (7) *will stay / are going to stay* with her in August. That's my holiday.

Tino: Nice! Listen. I have to go because (8) *I'll have / I'm going to have* lunch with Michelle in town. Do you want to come too?

Marta: Yeah, (9) *I'll come / I'm going to come*. Thanks!

1D A very bad journey

Vocabulary

Word Bank 3: Travel problems p. 66

Nouns: basketball, company, conference, flight, flood, hurricane, identification, journey, mobile, motorway, passenger, platform, programme, queue, ruins

Adjectives: ancient, elderly, enormous, lost, sick, worried

1 Complete with these words. There's one extra word.

> cancelled   jam   passport   platform
> queue   sick   ticket

1 We're waiting in a really long _____ . We'll be here for hours!

2 We're on the motorway but we're not moving. We're in an enormous traffic _____ .

3 Because of the hurricane in Mexico, they _____ our flight! It's not leaving today.

4 I forgot my _____ so I couldn't get on the plane because I didn't have any identification!

5 Barry doesn't like being in the car because he gets travel _____ .

6 Ahmed lost his _____ so he had to buy another one on the train.

2 Complete with these verbs.

> do (× 2)   play tennis   watch TV   work

1 What _____ at 9 o'clock this morning?
At 9? I can't remember! I think I was working.

2 Where _____ last week? I didn't see her in the office!
Jane? She was at a conference in Bogota.

3 _____ Bob _____ TV at midnight last night?
Yes, he was. He loves late night TV programmes.

4 _____ Cindy _____ at 8 this morning?
No, she usually plays in the afternoon.

5 What _____ Amy and San _____ yesterday afternoon?
They were probably shopping! They love it.

3 Rewrite the sentences. Change one verb into the Past continuous.

was snowing
1 It ~~snowed~~ when I woke up.

2 I met John when I studied at university.

3 People waited in the station because there weren't any trains.

4 I read about the floods when I ate breakfast.

5 We walked in the mountains for ages because we got lost.

6 Helen broke her arm when she played basketball.

4 (1.5) Circle the correct option. Listen and check.

Lost in Greece

About ten years ago, I [1] *travelled / was travelling* around Greece on holiday and I decided to go to Crete. I spent a week on the island because I [2] *wanted / was wanting* to visit the ancient ruins. One day, I went to the ruins of Phaestos and I [3] *took / was taking* the local bus. When I got there, only one or two other tourists [4] *walked / were walking* around the ruins. I took a lot of photographs. Finally, I went to the bus stop to wait for the bus home. An elderly man [5] *sat / was sitting* there and he started talking to me. After thirty minutes, I became worried because the bus was late and no one else [6] *waited / was waiting* there. Then the man said. "Oh no, this isn't the bus stop. The bus leaves from over there!" I saw my bus [7] *just left / was just leaving*! I missed it! [8] *I didn't know / wasn't knowing* what to do. Then, a taxi [9] *arrived / was arriving*. It already had somebody inside, but in Greece taxi drivers often take different people in the same car. So the driver took me to the hotel, but both the other passenger and I [10] *paid / were paying* the full price of the journey!

5 Match the sentences.

1 We texted you at 5.30 but you didn't reply.

2 I emailed you yesterday and you didn't reply.

3 Why weren't you in the office on Thursday?

4 I went to see you on Saturday but you were out.

a ☐ I was visiting another company.

b ☐ Sorry, my mobile wasn't working.

c ☐ I was spending the weekend with my parents.

d ☐ It's because I wasn't working on the computer.

Should I or shouldn't I?

Vocabulary

Word Bank 3: American and British English p. 66

Nouns: adventure, cell phone, direction, distance, downtown, freedom, item, mile, questionnaire, store, subway, vegetables

Adjectives: alone, independent, safe, violent

Adverbs: completely, partly, successfully

Verbs: climb, guess, lose, obey, protect

Expressions: all the time, on their own

---

1 Complete with these words. There's one extra word.

> adventure   freedom   independent   let
> protect   on his own   safe

My son is thirteen but he's already really
(1) _____ : he doesn't need help from
other people. I think it's because we gave him a
lot of (2) _____ when he was a child.
We (3) _____ him play outside and go to
new places (4) _____ . We live in a small
town and it's quite a (5) _____ place for
children. Everyone knows everyone. Of course, if
you live in a big place, you have to be more careful.
But also, you can't (6) _____ children all the
time, because they need a little danger in their lives.

2 Correct the sentences.

1 You should (to) do your homework before you go out tonight.

2 *We don't should go to the party tonight.*

3 *She shoulds phone her parents to tell them where she is.*

4 **They should studying for their exams.**

5 *Do I should get a taxi home?*

3 Match the sentence halves.

1 You should study in the library

2 You shouldn't eat chocolate all the time

3 You shouldn't put personal information on the Internet

4 You should study Chemistry at university

5 You shouldn't wear that coat

6 You should give the cat something to eat

a ☐ because it's bad for your teeth.

b ☐ because it looks terrible.

c ☐ because other people can use it.

d ☐ because you're good at science.

e ☐ because she's hungry.

f ☐ because it's quiet there.

4 Martin's always tired at school. Give his father advice with *should* + these phrases. Be careful with prepositions and articles.

> go / bed early
> spend all evening / Internet   have breakfast / mornings
> get up / same time every day
> go out / night during / week   watch TV late / night

1 *He should go to bed early.*

2 _____

3 _____

4 _____

5 _____

6 _____

5 (1.6) Dictation. Listen and write B's answers.

1 A: Parents shouldn't let young children play on their own.
   B: Yeah, _____ .

2 A: We don't think children should go out on school nights.
   B: _____

3 A: Children shouldn't climb trees because it's dangerous.
   B: _____

4 A: I don't think people should drive to work.
   B: _____

5 A: Everyone should learn English at school.
   B: _____

6 A: I don't think children should eat sweets or chocolate.
   B: _____

1F Location vacation!

Vocabulary

Word Bank 4: Going on holiday p. 67

Nouns: beauty, brochures, carriage, chase, countryside, dream, a double room, hill, location, nomination, railway, scene, series, survey, trip, wheel

Adjectives: amazing, colourful, comfortable, fantasy, ideal, including, limited, luxurious, magical, medieval, original, outdoor, whole, wonderful

Verbs: base on, follow   **Adverbs:** generally

Expressions: in general, I'm not feeling well. to go to bed late

---

Test yourself on Unit 1

1 Do these exercises to check your progress.

2 Count your **correct** answers.
Write the total number in the box.

Total: [ ] /50 correct answers

3 Try to understand your mistakes. If necessary,
- read the **Essential Grammar**, and/or
- look at the Student Book lesson again, or
- ask your teacher.

4 How do you feel after this unit? Tick (✓) a box.

👍👍☐ 👍☐ ✋☐ 👎☐ 👎👎☐

I can use articles correctly. (Lesson 1F)

1 Add two articles in the sentences.

1 Japan is ˄*a* large island in ˄*the* Pacific Ocean.

2 Yesterday I got text message from old friend.

3 Next train to Brussels leaves from Waterloo station at 12.30 in afternoon.

4 Joe! Can you help me? I can't find car keys. They were on table. Have you got them?

5 I'm going to shops because I need new pair of shoes.

6 Republic of Chile is long thin country.

2 Complete with *a*, *an*, *the* or no article. (Lesson 1F)

(1) *The* capital of (2) *O* Yemen is Sana'a, (3) *the* 'pearl of Arabia'. It's (4)____ amazing place to visit. It's one of (5)____ world's oldest cities, more than (6)____ 2,500 years old. There are (7)____ 103 mosques, 14 bathhouses and over 6,000 houses, all built before (8)____ 11th century. It is on (9)____ Unesco World Heritage List.

In (10)____ old town of (11)____ Sana'a it's like travelling back in (12)____ time. There are hundreds of (13)____ tall white houses, with (14)____ colourful windows. (15)____ small shops in (16)____ narrow streets of (17)____ old market are fantastic and full of (18)____ beautiful jewellery. You don't need (19)____ map or (20)____ guide. Just walk around, get lost and enjoy (21)____ atmosphere. It's (22)____ incredible and (23)____ people are really friendly too.

I can make questions. (Lesson 1A)

3 Complete the negative questions.

1 My brother doesn't like U2. (why?)
Why *doesn't he like them?*

2 I'm not going to sleep tonight.
Why _____

3 I wasn't at school yesterday.
Why _____

4 Ben didn't do it.
Why _____

5 The students didn't do their homework.
Why _____

4 Write questions for these answers.

1 _____ ?
We stayed in a youth hostel.

2 _____ ?
It was hot and sunny all the time.

3 _____ ?
No, that's not my book. It's yours.

4 _____ ?
I'm not at school because I'm not feeling well.

5 _____ ?
It was beautiful. The Eiffel Tower was amazing and we loved the Louvre.

6 _____ ?
I went with my brother and his wife.

I can use the Present tenses. (Lesson 1B)

5 Circle the correct option.

1 We *never take / are never taking* the bus to school.

2 What *do you do / are you doing* at the moment?

3 *He usually walks / He's usually walking* home.

4 I'm not at school because *I go / I'm going* to the dentist.

5 *It rains / It's raining* and I haven't got an umbrella.

6 She rarely *gets / is rarely getting* the underground.

7 My sister *does / 's doing* a PhD at Berlin University.

I can talk about the future. (Lesson 1C)

6 Match the sentences to the responses.

1 Somebody needs to go to the meeting but I'm not in the office tomorrow.

2 Can one of you go and get some more eggs? We've only got two.

3 Dan sent us an email asking if we could bring some music to the party.

4 Do you have time to prepare some food for lunch?

5 Celia doesn't know where we are.

6 It's Katya's birthday tomorrow.

a ☐ OK, I'll go, Mum. Do you need anything else?

b ☐ Sure. I'll make a salad.

c ☐ I know. I'm going to get her a present today.

d ☐ Yeah, I've read it. I'm going to take a CD.

e ☐ It's OK. I'll ask my boss to go.

f ☐ I'll send her a text message.

I can use the Past continuous. (Lesson 1D)

7 Complete with the correct form of the verbs.

1 I _was riding_ my bike to work when I saw Jill. *(ride, see)*

2 We _____ a film at the cinema when suddenly Al's mobile _____ ringing. *(watch, start)*

3 Kim _____ Darren when she _____ for a train ticket. *(meet, queue)*

4 The man _____ he was a police officer but he _____ a uniform. *(say, not / wear)*

5 We _____ to the British Museum but it started raining so we _____ for lunch on the way. *(go, stop)*

6 When we _____ to the museum, lots of people _____ outside! *(get, wait)*

I can give advice with **should / shouldn't.** (Lesson 1E)

8 Give advice with *should / shouldn't.*

1 That apple is very old. You ___*shouldn't eat it*___ .

2 This book is really good. You _____.

3 Your hair is very long. You _____.

4 Smoking is really bad for you. You _____.

5 If you've got a bad headache you _____ aspirin.

6 When you're driving you _____ any alcohol.

7 There's a great exhibition at the museum. You _____.

I can say 100 more words in English. (Lessons 1A–1F)

9 Cover the words and test yourself on …

1 (WB) The weather (p.64)

Can you remember all the words and phrases?

2 (WB) The verb *get* (p.65)

Can you remember the five meanings of *get* and the 14 phrases?

3 (WB) Travel problems (p.66)

Can you remember the 10 phrases?

4 (WB) American and British English (p.66)

Can you remember the 10 pairs of phrases?

5 (WB) Going on holiday (p.67)

Can you remember the 12 phrases with *go* and the other 8 phrases?

6 (Phrasebook 1) (p.77) Look only at your translations.

Can you remember the phrases in English?

Which film is better?

Vocabulary

Word Bank 5: Adjectives p. 68
Nouns: actress, director, ending, genre, pity, reality TV
Adjectives: attractive, average, dark, successful   **Verbs:** die, practice, rent
Adverbs: definitely, forever, regularly   **Expressions:** when I was little, Phew!

1 Find eight adjectives to describe films.

X	R	P	X	D	R	K	F	Y	E	W
J	O	I	A	V	I	O	L	E	N	T
E	M	Q	T	O	G	J	R	P	J	E
W	A	Z	F	U	N	N	Y	Q	O	X
O	N	K	Y	X	B	B	D	Y	Y	C
T	T	S	E	R	I	O	U	S	A	I
Y	I	J	H	K	Y	E	U	F	B	T
H	C	O	T	A	O	G	W	Y	L	I
K	S	T	U	P	I	D	C	Z	E	N
G	X	A	D	W	M	R	M	G	Q	G
P	O	W	E	R	F	U	L	V	Q	G

2 (**2.1**) Listen to two people comparing films with their sequels.

1 Does she prefer *The Godfather* (1972) or *The Godfather Part II* (1974)?

2 Did he prefer *Raiders of the Lost Ark* (1981) or *Indiana Jones and the Kingdom of the Crystal Skull* (2008)?

3 Listen again and find the comparative of these adjectives.

difficult	exciting	funny	good	old
recent	romantic	successful	violent	

4 Correct the sentences.

1 *The sequel is* ~~*scaryer*~~ *scarier than the original film.*

2 My brother's apartment biger than mine.

3 *My new laptop is more powerful as my old one.*

4 *The trains are more crowd in summer than in winter.*

5 **Your boss is seriouser than mine.**

6 *The Lord of the Rings is longer The Hobbit.*

5 Complete with the comparative adjectives.

1 The Ferrari is _faster_ than the Toyota. (fast)

2 Is the underground _____ than the bus? (expensive)

3 Special effects are _____ today than in the past. (realistic)

4 This beach is _____ than the beach near my house! (bad)

5 I'm _____ in my new job than I was in my last job. (happy)

6 Football is _____ than rugby. (popular)

6 Complete the sentences with *Gina* and *Ami*.

Name	Gina	Ami
Age	25	23
Height	165cm	166cm
English	Excellent	OK
Home	House with three bedrooms	One bedroom apartment
Hair	Black	Blond

1 _____ is younger than _____ .

2 _____ is shorter than _____ .

3 _____ speaks better English than _____ .

4 _____ lives in a smaller house than _____ .

5 _____ has darker hair than _____ .

Have you read *Duma Key*?

Vocabulary

Word Bank 13: Irregular verbs p. 76

Nouns: accident, author, autobiography, bestseller, biography, book cover, bubble, critic, education, health, interview, novel, novelist, puzzle, screenplay, subtitles, text message, vehicle

Adjectives: below, best-selling, brilliant, current, fiction, literary, major, married, online, several

Verbs: praise, publish, swap, taste   **Adverbs:** internationally

Expressions: sense of humour, It's brilliant!

---

1 Complete the puzzle. What's the word in grey?

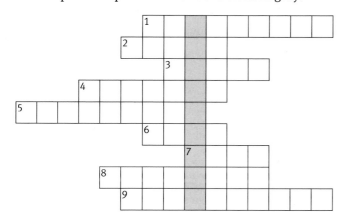

1 When you watch a film in a foreign language, you see these words at the bottom of the screen.

2 You can read about Batman or Superman in these.

3 This is a book with a long, continuous story. It's fiction: not real.

4 On the Internet you don't read on paper, you read on a m…

5 There's a new one every day. It tells you what's happening in the world, e.g. *The Times, Le Monde*.

6 Things you see at theatres like *Macbeth* or *Hamlet*.

7 A text with short lines and a very nice sound. You may write one because you love somebody.

8 You read this when you want to buy something, e.g. a holiday. It has information about the products.

9 This book helps you learn a foreign language because it's easier to read than normal books (two words: 4, 6).

2 Write the past participles of these verbs. Write S (same) in the past tense or D (different).

1 begin	*begun* D	7 make	_____ __
2 drive	_____ __	8 read	_____ __
3 go	_____ __	9 send	_____ __
4 grow	_____ __	10 think	_____ __
5 know	_____ __	11 win	_____ __
6 lose	_____ __	12 write	_____ __

3 Write true Present perfect sentences about yourself.

1 eat sushi _____ *I've eaten sushi many times.*_____

2 see Spielberg films _____

3 be to Cairo _____

4 fly in a plane _____

5 do the homework _____

6 go skiing _____

4 (**2.2**) Circle the correct options. Listen and check.

Bill Bryson was born in Des Moines, Iowa and grew up in the USA. He [(1)] *moved / has moved* to the UK in 1977 and during the 1970s and 1980s, he [(2)] *worked / has worked* for newspapers such as 'The Times' and 'The Independent'. He [(3)] *went / has gone* back to the US in 1995 but he [(4)] *now returned / has now returned* to the UK, where he lives with his family.

During his career, Bill Bryson [(5)] *wrote / has written* several best-selling travel books, such as 'The Lost Continent' and 'Notes from a Big Country'. His books [(6)] *sold / have sold* hundreds of thousands of copies because they're funny and very original. However, he [(7)] *did / has done* much more than write about travel. He [(8)] *also published / has also published* books on science, 'A Short History of Nearly Everything', as well as a biography of Shakespeare. In 2005, he [(9)] *became / has become* Chancellor of Durham University in England.

5 (**2.3**) Order the dialogue, 1–7. Listen and check.

a ☐ Marcia. She liked it too.

b ☐ I went to the cinema with her last week. We saw *Mamma Mia*. Have you seen it?

c ☐ Yeah, it's brilliant! I saw it yesterday.

d ☐ *Mamma Mia*? Of course! I saw it with you!

e ☐ Who did you go with?

f ☐ *1* Have you seen the new Steven Spielberg film?

g ☐ Oh, sorry. I forgot!

A spider for breakfast?

Vocabulary

Word Bank 5: Adjectives p. 68

Nouns: applicant, bat, candidate, contestant, details, extrovert, fan, joke, mix, producer, spider

Adjectives: aggressive, boring, calm, energetic, exciting, gorgeous, tired, unusual

Verbs: seem, suppose, take part in, vote

Expressions: I was quite shocked. Well, I have some news. That's not true.

1 Order the personality adjectives.

1 When Louise went into the Big Brother house nobody spoke to her. They were really _____ . (*redynfinul*)

2 She was really polite but everybody was _____ to her. (*dure*)

3 Maybe it's because she's beautiful and naturally _____. They were afraid she was going to win easily. (*ottexerv*)

4 One contestant, Jojo, was really _____ with her. She thought he was going to start a fight with him. (*sageergivs*)

5 But an older contestant, Andy, is really _____ . He loves to chat and he made friends with her. (*kevalitat*)

6 Andy told Louise 'Don't worry. Jojo gets angry easily but he's _____ really. He won't hurt you. (*teleng*)

7 In the end, Louise didn't win. Andy won because he was _____ with people of all ages. (*opplaru*)

2 Rewrite using *not / enough*.

1 I'm afraid you're too late to see Dr Chan. She's gone.

You mean ___*I wasn't early enough to see her*___ .

2 You're too young to watch this film. You have to be over 18.

You mean _____ .

3 The children are too weak to carry those huge bags.

You mean _____ .

3 Rewrite using *too*.

1 I'm not fresh enough to do the homework.

You mean ___*you're too tired to do the homework*___

2 It isn't late enough to go to bed. It's only 7.30.

You mean _____ .

3 The city centre isn't near enough to walk. Let's get a bus.

You mean _____ .

4 Match the beginning to the end of the quotes. Do you agree with them?

1 Earth provides **enough** to satisfy every man's need,

2 A man must be big **enough** to admit his mistakes, smart **enough** to profit from them,

3 When you know what you want, and want it bad **enough**,

4 He who knows that **enough** is **enough**

a ☐ and strong enough to correct them. (John C Maxwell)

b ☐ will always have enough. (Lao Tsu)

c ☐ but not every man's greed. (Mahatma Gandhi)

d ☐ you will find a way to get it." (Jim Rohn)

5 **(2.4)** Put *too* × 3 and *enough* × 3 in the correct place in the dialogue. Listen and check.

Ros: Have you seen this advert for a new reality TV show? You have to live on a desert island for a month with ten other people.

Kim: Yeah, I saw the advert but I'm ^too^ old to do something like that. You have to be under 30, and I'm 31!

Ros: Well, I have some news. Trisha Boswell's applying for the show.

Kim: Trisha! She's not pretty to go on TV. They want really beautiful people.

Ros: She looks great! I think it's a good idea.

Kim: But she's serious.

Ros: She's not serious – she's great fun.

Kim: OK, but she isn't funny to go on a TV show. You're funnier. You should apply!

Ros: Me? No, I'm not confident and I'm busy! No way!

Do you love your computer?

Vocabulary

Word Bank 6: Computers p. 69

Nouns: addict, comment, device, disk, equipment, gamer, geek, hacker, hard disk, hardware, immigrant, laptop, modem, monitor, parts, pirate, prison, profile, programmer, sat nav, score, security

Adjectives: compulsive, confusing, illegal, particular, passionate, sophisticated, technical, up-to-date

Verbs: break into, build, cause, complain, connect, cost, download, keep, lend, touch, upgrade

Expressions: They are really annoying.

1 Complete the puzzle.

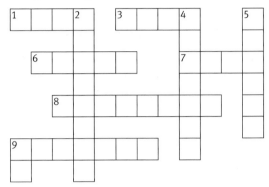

ACROSS

1 You click on this to go to another web page.

3 If you have a ... connection, you can connect to the Internet without using cables.

6 To ... information is to enter information by typing (two words: 3, 2).

7 These are emails from people you don't know. They are really annoying and you can receive hundreds!

8 To take something off the Internet and put it onto your computer.

9 To improve your computer by adding new hardware or software.

DOWN

2 This has lots of letters. You press them to make words on your computer.

4 To put a new program on your computer.

5 You can use the ... control to turn on the TV without leaving your chair.

9 Before you go online you have to start ... your computer.

2 (**2.5**) Dictation. Listen and complete with comparatives and superlatives of the adjectives.

1 **A:** I'm _____ student in the class!

   B: No, you're not. I'm _____ than you. Look I got 100% in my last test. What did you get?

   A: Oh, only 50%. You may be right. *clever*

2 **C:** I hate this country. It's always raining. It's the _____ place in the world!

   D: What? Your country is _____ than this one! You come from England!

   C: Yes, right. Maybe I should be more positive. *wet*

3 **E:** My new flat's _____ than my old one!

   F: Really? But your old flat was really cold and the location was terrible.

   E: But this one's much noisier, more expensive and yesterday I even saw a rat! Ugh! It's the _____ flat in the city! *bad*

3 Look at the pictures. Complete with superlatives of the adjectives.

1 Jim's got _____ screen. *(thin)*

2 Don's got _____ computer. *(large)*

3 Jim's got _____ hardware. *(modern)*

4 Don's got _____ printer. *(old)*

5 Jim's got _____ hard drive. *(powerful)*

6 Don's got _____ Internet connection. *(slow)*

4 (**2.6**) Dictation. Listen and complete the webpage.

The Internet is the (1) _____ thing made by human beings. The (2) _____ language on the Internet is English. It is used by 30% of all Internet users, but the language with the (3) _____ growth is Arabic. The Internet is also the (4) _____ thing on earth made by people. This is because it uses telephone lines, with millions of kilograms of metal wire and other cables. So it's amazing to think that the Internet is so young: Microsoft, the (5) _____ software company in the world, didn't have a website until 1991!

Have you ever volunteered?

Vocabulary

Word Bank 7: Useful verbs p. 70
Nouns: beginning, coincidence, elephant, experience, hunter, orphanage, project, volunteer
Adjectives: crazy, delicious, excellent, rewarding, wild   **Verbs:** employ, imagine, volunteer
Adverbs: ever, exactly   **Expressions:** Wow! from natural causes

1 Complete with vowels. Circle thirteen animals.

horse f_sh_l_ph_ntsp_id_rd_lph_
nch_ck_nd_gc_tsn_ _lt_g_rr_tt_rt_
_h_mst_r

2 Complete with the correct form of *make* or *do*.

1 I can't come because I _____ the ironing.

2 They had to _____ a very difficult decision.

3 Tony _____ something crazy at the concert yesterday.

4 We need to _____ some exercise.

5 This is the third time I _____ this journey.

3 Match 1–5 with a–e. There's one extra.

1 I gave up *Robinson Crusoe* after three chapters.

2 My new car cost €10,000.

3 We were on a boat in Mexico and there were loads of whales in the sea.

4 It was −30° when we were in Moscow.

5 The team lost 6–1.

a ☐ It's the most expensive thing I've ever bought.

b ☐ They're the worst players we've ever had.

c ☐ It was the coldest place I've ever been.

d ☐ It was the hardest thing I've ever done.

e ☐ It's the most boring book I've ever read.

f ☐ They were the most amazing animals I've ever seen.

4 Circle the correct option.

1 This is the *four / fourth* time I've called you!

2 It's the *longer / longest* journey they've ever done.

3 This is the most interesting book *I've ever read / I'm ever reading*.

4 She's the most famous person I've ever *met / meet*.

5 This is the nicest room I've ever *stayed / stayed in*!

5 Read the situations. Use the words to write a superlative + *ever* + present perfect sentence.

1 Lots of people died in the movie. *(violent film)*
It was the most violent film I've ever seen.

2 We danced all night at your party. *(good / party)*

_____

3 My grandpa is 95. *(old / person / meet)*

_____

4 The exam was for four hours! *(long exam / take)*

_____

5 Sue volunteers in a hospital. *(rewarding thing / do)*

_____

6 They left the US and moved to Mexico. *(difficult decision / make)*

_____

6 Match stories 1–4 to the animals. There's one extra.

an eagle ____   a frog ____   a tiger ____
an elephant ____   a monkey ____

1 I saw them in Japan. They like to go in the hot water and wash themselves. They look and act just like people with their little red faces, and their tiny hands. They're the funniest animals I've ever seen.

2 I was on holiday in India and I was in a jeep in the jungle. When we stopped the car, we saw one, watching us. It was in a tree and it was black and red. It was really close to us and it was enormous. It was the most beautiful animal I've ever seen.

3 We rode on one when we were on holiday in Sri Lanka. There was a local man who told it where to go and it carried all three of us through the jungle. It was the most incredible experience I've ever had.

4 I was on a walking holiday in the USA, in the mountains and I had my new digital camera. I wanted to take a picture of the sky. When I turned on my camera, I saw this huge bird and I quickly took the picture. I was lucky and it's the best photo I've ever taken.

Special memories

Vocabulary

Word Bank 7: Useful verbs p. 70

Nouns: chance, crowd, encore, event, hit, memory, metre, runner, stage, track

Adjectives: against, boiling, disappointed, lucky, nice, superb

Verbs: appear, boo, care, catch, cheer, clap, rain, run, worth

Adverbs: afterwards, carefully, incredibly   **Expressions:** Ow! Ouch! Uh-huh!

Test yourself on Unit 2

1 Do these exercises to check your progress.

2 Count your **correct** answers.
Write the total number in the box.

Total: ⬜ /40 correct answers

3 Try to understand your mistakes. If necessary,
- read the **Essential Grammar**, and/or
- look at the Student Book lesson again, or
- ask your teacher.

4 How do you feel after this unit? Tick (✓) a box.

👍👍⬜ 👍⬜ ✊⬜ 👎⬜ 👎👎⬜

I can use so / such ... that. (Lesson 2F)

1 Complete with *so* or *such*.

1 The film was _____ boring that I left the cinema after ten minutes.

2 It was _____ a long journey that I fell asleep on the plane.

3 There were _____ many people on the train that it was impossible to sit down.

4 We started surfing at 8 a.m. It was _____ fun that I stayed in the water all day.

5 It was _____ wet on holiday that we couldn't do anything except stay in and eat!

6 It was _____ an early flight that we had to get up at 4 a.m.

2 Add one word to each sentence.

| an | hot | so | such | than | that |

1 It was so in the tent that I couldn't sleep.

2 It was such a nice day we decided to go for a picnic.

3 The restaurant had good food that we ate there every day.

4 It was such interesting museum that we went there twice.

5 The countryside was beautiful that I took almost a hundred photos!

6 The weather in Northern Europe is so much nicer in summer winter.

I can compare things. (Lesson 2A)

3 Write comparative sentences with the adjectives.

1 Joe is 28. Danni is 31. *(young)*
Joe is younger than Danni.

2 Sam's flat is 65m². Tina's flat is 100m². *(big)*

3 My laptop's quick. Yours is slow. *(powerful)*

4 The flight to New York's five hours but to L. A. it's eight hours. *(long)*

5 I got 85% in the English exam but only 32% in the French exam. *(easy)*

6 Maths is no problem but nobody understands Chemistry. *(difficult)*

I can use the Past simple and the Present perfect.
(Lesson 2B)

4 Circle the correct option.

1 *We went / We've been* to the beach yesterday.

2 We're having sushi tonight. *I never ate / I've never eaten* it before.

3 Since John left university *he had / he's had* seven jobs.

4 Sheila *lived / has lived* in Thailand from 2002 to 2008.

5 I'm reading the new Stephen King book. I *didn't finish / haven't finished* it yet.

6 My parents *gave / have given* me a new jumper for my last birthday.

I can use too and enough. (Lesson 2C)

5 Order the sentences. Add *too* or *enough*.

1 serious / think / don't / they / you're
They don't think you're serious enough.

2 noisy / my / neighbours / are

_____

3 He's / see / that / old / film / to / not

_____

4 go / TV / Alice / to / on / is / shy

_____

5 aren't / win / you / good / competition / to / the

_____

6 you're / university / go / to / to / young /

_____

I can use superlatives. (Lesson 2D)

6 Write superlative sentences with these adjectives.

| aggressive | expensive | fat | friendly | large | small |

1 Tony is _____ dog.

2 Brutus is _____ dog.

3 Dermot is _____ dog.

4 Petal is _____ dog.

5 Gordo is _____ dog.

6 Mimi is _____ dog.

I can use the Present perfect with superlatives.
(Lesson 2E)

7 Match the sentences to the responses.

1 I didn't understand the text at all.

2 He arrived with an enormous bunch of flowers.

3 I worked in Borneo in an orphanage for baby orangutans.

4 The flight was only €1!

5 U2 played for three hours without a break.

6 I started the meal but I couldn't finish it.

a ☐ It was the most rewarding thing I've ever done.

b ☐ It was the most difficult thing I've ever read.

c ☐ It was the most beautiful present I've ever had.

d ☐ It was the most disgusting thing I've ever eaten.

e ☐ It was the best concert I've ever seen.

f ☐ It was the cheapest ticket I've ever bought.

I can say 100 more words in English. (Lessons 2A–2F)

8 Cover the words and test yourself on ...

1 **WB** Adjectives (p.68)

Can you pronounce the 16 adjectives correctly?

2 **WB** Irregular verbs (p.76)

How many past participles can you remember?

3 **WB** Adjectives (p.68)

Can you remember and pronounce the six pairs of opposite adjectives correctly?

4 **WB** Computers (p.69)

Can you say the 17 words and phrases?

5 **WB** Useful verbs (p.70)

Cover the words in Exercise 1. Can you remember the 9 phrases?

6 **Phrasebook 2** (p.77) Look only at your translations.

Can you remember the phrases in English?

Learn English the modern way

Vocabulary

Word Bank 8: Verbs, Adjectives and prepositions p. 71

Nouns: arrangement, board, century, classmate, headphones, icon, introduction, learner, natural wonder, newsletter, obligation, pleasure, skills, tree   **Adjectives:** busy, foreign, man-made, virtual

Verbs: interrupt, link up, log on, plant, print out, register, suggest   **Adverbs:** abroad, equally, mainly

Expressions: Can you help me? What's the problem? What's wrong with ... ? It's too late now.

1 Complete what the teacher says with these words.

> down   in   off   on   up

1 We don't need to use the computer. You can turn it _____ .

2 I want everyone to stand _____ and come to the front of the class.

3 You need a password before you can log _____ to the Wifi service.

4 I'm tired. Will you get me a chair so I can sit _____ ?

5 We've nearly finished. Now fill _____ this form.

2 (**3.1**) Dictation. Listen and complete.

A A: Excuse me. (1)_____ you help me, please? I'm trying to (1)_____ _____ this (1)_____.

B: What's the problem?

A: Well, I have to (2)_____ _____ the 'Registration number'. But I haven't got (1)_____.

B: It's the same number that you use to (3)_____ _____ to our computer system.

A: OK, thanks. That's easy _____, even for me!

B C: Oh no! All my paper's falling on the floor.

D: Don't worry. I'll (4)_____ it _____ for you. But ... Hey! What's (4)_____ with the printer? How many pages are you (5)_____ _____?

C: Er ... about a hundred.

D: A hundred! Are you _____ a whole book?

C: No! They're _____ for my band's concert next week. I'm going to (6)_____ them _____ all the noticeboards in the school.

3 Complete with *must* or *mustn't*.

1 All swimmers _____ wear a swimming cap.

2 You _____ run around the pool.

3 You _____ jump into the pool.

4 Parents _____ look after young children at all times.

5 Everyone _____ leave the pool by 6 p.m.

6 You _____ use the pool if there is no lifeguard.

4 (**3.2**) Circle the correct option. Listen and check.

Dom: I really want to learn Italian but it's too late now. You (1) *have to / don't have to* start young to learn a language.

Ana: That's not true! You (2) *have to / don't have to* be young. I started learning English when I was 30 and I speak it fluently now.

Dom: So what (3) *do / don't* I have to do?

Ana: To start, buy a book and study it at home. In the beginning, you (4) *have to / don't have to* sit down and just learn some words. Then you need to find a teacher.

Dom: I don't have time to do a course.

Ana: You (5) *have to / don't have to* do a course with other students. You could find a private teacher to help you.

Dom: I don't know. I mean, I just want to learn Italian. I (6) *have to / don't have to* learn it for my job.

Ana: Well, I think you should try. Yes, you (7) *have to / don't have to* work hard but it is fun too!

5 Two options are correct. Cross out the wrong one.

1 In the UK you *have to / must / ~~should~~* drive on the left.

2 You *mustn't / haven't to / can't* go into the building before 7 a.m.

3 Mineko *must / have to / should* study for her English exam.

4 I think people *has to / have to / must* vote in elections.

5 The homework is optional: you *don't need to / don't have to / mustn't* do it.

6 You really *have to / must / mustn't* lose some weight or you won't live long.

3B A new life

1 Two options are correct. Cross out the wrong one.

1 They've lived in New York for
   a five years.   b a year.   c ~~1999.~~

2 He's been in the house
   a for 8 o'clock.   b since 8 o'clock.   c all day.

3 I haven't seen Tom
   a today.   b for a year.   c last year.

4 We've had broadband here since
   a 2007.   b months.   c November.

5 You haven't stopped playing the computer
   a since hours!   b for hours!   c since 6 o'clock!

6 We haven't heard from Chen for
   a November.   b years.   c seven months.

7 We've waited for this bus
   a too long.   b for ages.   c since a long time.

2 Complete with the verbs and *since* or *for*.

1 I *haven't spoken* to my parents ___since___ Christmas!
   (not speak)

2 I _____ to work by bus _____ my first
   day there. *(go)*

3 Lou _____ in a plane _____ ten years .
   (not fly)

4 Nobody _____ trousers like that _____
   the 1980s! *(wear)*

5 It _____ here _____ weeks. *(not rain)*

6 We _____ any electricity _____ a couple
   of hours. *(not have)*

3 Write Present perfect sentences for the situations.

1 Al's on the train. He got on at 6 a.m.

   Al's been on the train since 6 a.m.

2 Tove lives in Stuttgart. She moved there in 1995.

   _____

3 Lucy doesn't drink coffee. She stopped drinking it
   seven months ago.

   _____

4 My dad still drives his old Volvo. He bought it in
   1991 and he says it's great!

   _____

5 We don't sell videos. We stopped selling them in
   the 1990s!

   _____

4 Read the article. Then complete with *Anna* or *Noel*.

Anna Seth

Anna lives in Beijing. She moved here
from India twenty years ago to teach
English and loved it immediately.
She's been to every corner of China
and really likes each place she's
visited. She studied Chinese and
now she's fluent. Since she arrived,
the country has become much more industrial, the
cities have grown and English has become much more
popular. And she has so many students that she's
opened her own language school.

Noel Coffey

Noel came to Beijing from Ireland last
month. It's his first time abroad and
he's finding life difficult. He's living
in a hotel because it's really hard to
find an apartment. Not speaking the
language makes it worse, although
he can read some Chinese letters.
He teaches in a language school but it's his first job so
he has to prepare lessons all weekend. His new Chinese
friends want to show him lots of places. He doesn't
have time now but he will soon.

1 _____ has travelled all over China.

2 _____ has only been in Beijing for four weeks.

3 _____ has learned to read a little Chinese.

4 _____ has learnt to speak Chinese.

5 _____ has had to work at weekends.

6 _____ has started a business.

5 (**3.3**) Imagine their answers. Listen and check.

1 **Anna:** Where have you been in China?

2   What changes have you seen in China?

3   Has your school been successful?

4 **Noel:** Have you been to Asia before?

5   Has your job been difficult?

6   Have you made any Chinese friends?

How good is your vocabulary?

Vocabulary

Word Bank 2: The verb *get* p. 65

Nouns: alarm clock, bottle, crossword, opposite, progress, remote control, technique, tongue, zebra

Adjectives: active, definite, native, well-known   **Verbs:** define, increase, stress

Adverbs: actively, especially, passively

Other: everybody, everything, everywhere, somebody, something, somewhere, nobody, nothing, nowhere

Expressions: Come on! It's a difficult one! No, not that. It's on the tip of my tongue!

1 Complete the crossword puzzle.

ACROSS

1 This is somebody who works in fashion shows, wearing beautiful clothes.

5 It's somewhere you go when you want to see a film.

6 It's something you do in your mouth.

7 It's the opposite of *closed*.

9 I promise I've spoken _____ nobody about your secrets!

10 This is a book which you write in every day with your personal ideas and thoughts.

DOWN

1 It's somewhere you can visit to see important objects from the past.

2 It's somebody you go to see when you don't feel well.

3 That view is amazing. I've never _____ anything like it.

4 It's somebody that serves food in a restaurant.

8 It's the opposite of *start* or *begin*.

2 (**3.4**) Dictation. Listen and complete.

1 A: The nightclub's empty!
B: Yeah. _____.

2 A: Have you found that letter?
B: No, _____ !

3 A: Why are we going to the supermarket?
B: Because _____.

4 A: I've lost my keys!
B: Don't _____.

5 A: Can you help me with my Chemistry homework?
B: _____.

6 A: I've got an e-mail in German and I don't understand it.
B: You _____.

3 Match the sentence halves. There's one extra.

1 An iPod is something

2 A caiman is an animal

3 A password is something

4 A kangaroo is an animal

5 A hacker is somebody

6 A dishwasher is something

7 An actor is somebody

a ☐ that looks like a little crocodile.

b ☐ that plays music.

c ☐ who illegally enters computer systems.

d ☐ that cleans plates and cups.

e ☐ who works in the theatre.

f ☐ that comes from Australia.

4 Correct the two mistakes in each sentence.

1 *Printer is somewhere that makes paper copies of computer files.*

2 *Everybody know that your Sam's girlfriend.*

3 *I know no thing about computer.*

4 *A wetsuit is someone who you wear when you're surfing.*

5 *A shark is animal that live in the sea.*

6 *Janine's girl which met us at the station.*

5 (**3.5**) Complete the dialogue. Listen and check.

Roger: OK. Let's play Password. First clue. It's a difficult one. You'll (1) n _____ g __ __ !

Denise: Come on! Come on!

Roger: OK. It's an animal that has a very big mouth. It's a bird ...

Denise: Oh, I know (2) w ____ y __ m ____ . It's a pelican.

Roger: No, not that. It's a bird that has brown feathers and it can't fly.

Denise: Penguin? No, wait. Er ... I know it. I know it. It's on the (3) t __ __ o __ m __ tongue.

Roger: Yes?

Denise: Sorry, it's (4) g ____ . I don't know.

Roger: Yes, you do. It (5) b _____ with *K*.

Denise: K? A bird?

Roger: Do you (6) g ____ u __?

Denise: I know – it's from New Zealand, isn't it? A kiwi!

A holiday with a difference

Vocabulary

Word Bank 9: Driving p. 72

Nouns: beach, bridge, crossroads, exit, fashion, luxury, mate, motorway, scenery, tourism

Adjectives: European, fantastic, free-time

Expressions: We're nearly there. Good work. Now what?

1 Correct the two mistakes in each sentence.

1 We're so happy *as* ~~so~~ they ~~are~~. *(as ... are)*

2 He as intelligent like you.

3 **The sequel isn't so well as the original film.**

4 Maths not as more interesting as History.

5 My dessert isn't as tastier as your.

6 **The winter isn't as colder like last year.**

2 Read the brochure. Complete the sentences with *as ... as* + the adjective.

This year's cruise holidays!

	Patagonia	The Norwegian Fjords	The Greek Islands
Length	2 weeks	14 days	10 days
Cost	€2,459	€1,450	€1,450
Accommodation	★★★★★	★★★★	★★★★
Cruise ship	La Isla Negra Built 1988 Size: 90m Cars? No	The Trondheim Built 2004 Size: 56m Cars? No	The Penelope Built 2004 Size: 45m Cars? Max 20

1 The holiday in Patagonia _____ the one in Norway. *(long)*

2 The cruise in Norway _____ the one in Greece. *(expensive)*

3 The accommodation in Greece _____ the accommodation in Patagonia. *(comfortable)*

4 The Penelope _____ the Trondheim. *(old)*

5 The Trondheim _____ La Isla Negra. *(large)*

6 La Isla Negra _____ The Penelope for people taking their car. *(convenient)*

3 Order the letters to make traffic words.

1 This street is closed because of the _____ . *(woorrskad)*

2 There's a _____ over the river. *(giberd)*

3 You can drive down a _____ which goes through the mountains. *(lentun)*

4 At the _____ you can turn left, right or go straight on. *(nobaudurot)*

5 If you want to walk over the road, use the pedestrian _____ over there. *(sognircs)*

6 To get from Birmingham to Manchester quickly, use the _____ . *(woyartom)*

7 You must turn left at the traffic _____ . *(sithgl)*

8 Which _____ do we need for London? *(xeit)*

4 Circle the correct option.

1 Take the next junction *away / off* the motorway. We'll leave it there.

2 Go *past / down* the hill to the bottom.

3 Turn left *at / in* the crossroads.

4 We need the next turning *on / in* the right.

5 The bridge is very low. Only cars smaller than 2m can go *under / down* it.

5 (3.6) Order the dialogue. Listen and check.

a ☐1 We're lost, aren't we?

b ☐ Braintree Avenue. Well, we're on River Street. Are we a long way away?

c ☐ Isn't there? Look, we need the Red Lion Hotel. Can you find it?

d ☐ OK, I've found it. We need Braintree Avenue.

e ☐ No, no, I know where we are. But ... have you got the map?

f ☐ River Street? Then we're nearly there. Look, at the roundabout take the first exit.

g ☐ Yes, I have, but look, Tim. We're coming up to a roundabout, and there isn't one on the map!

h ☐ I see it! Here we are! Thanks, Donna.

i ☐ First exit. Right. Now what?

j ☐ Go up the hill and turn right at the crossroads. The Red Lion Hotel is there.

High earners

Vocabulary

Word Bank 13: Irregular verbs p. 76
Nouns: cartoonist, celebrity, classical music, clue, guitar, guitarist, painter, photographer, profession, sex symbol, singer, winner
Adjectives: best-known, country and western, dead   **Verbs:** design, draw, paint, record, rhyme, shoot
Expressions: Everyone knows that.

1 Find eight professions.

X	W	S	C	I	E	N	T	I	S	T	X
P	H	O	T	O	G	R	A	P	H	E	R
W	E	F	S	X	B	K	Y	H	N	X	Q
Y	R	F	Q	V	G	Z	F	E	S	L	M
G	U	I	T	A	R	I	S	T	I	W	U
R	M	U	S	V	R	N	B	J	N	L	S
Q	Z	P	A	I	N	T	E	R	G	Z	I
K	Q	K	B	E	F	U	X	Q	E	F	C
X	A	C	T	O	R	H	V	H	R	S	I
C	A	R	T	O	O	N	I	S	T	Y	A
T	N	S	K	M	B	X	V	Y	U	Z	N

2 Complete the questions with these verbs. There's one extra. Then match to the right answer.

> direct   discover   invent   paint
> star   wear   write

1 Who _____ the *Sunflowers*?

2 Who _____ the 2008 film *Slumdog Millionaire*?

3 Who _____ gravity?

4 Who _____ the book *Da Vinci Code*?

5 Which 2008 film _____ Sean Penn as a politician?

6 Which British pop singer _____ crazy glasses and clothes in the 1980s?

☐ Bono   ☐ Danny Boyle   ☐ Dan Brown

☐ Elton John   ☐ Milk   ☐ Isaac Newton

☐ Van Gogh

3 Circle the subject. Underline the object. Then cross out the wrong option.

1 Who *sang / did they sing* 'Come as you are'?

2 Where *worked you / did you work* last year?

3 Who *draws / does he draw* 'The Simpsons' cartoons*?*

4 Who *made / did he make* a work of art from a dead shark?

5 How much *earned U2 / did U2 earn* last year?

6 Which famous writer *died / did he die* in 1616 in Stratford-upon-Avon?

4 (**3.7**) Do the quiz. Listen and check your answers.

The 2008 Quiz

In 2008...

1 ... who won the Best Actor Oscar?
   a Javier Bardem
   b Daniel Day-Lewis
   c Forest Whitaker

2 ... who recorded the album *Perfect Symmetry*?
   a Keane
   b Coldplay
   c Muse

3 ... who won The Australian Open women's tennis championship?
   a Serena Williams
   b Ana Ivanović
   c Maria Sharapova

4 ... who broke the record for the men's 100 metres at the Olympic Games?
   a Asafa Powell
   b Tyson Gay
   c Usain Bolt

5 ... who didn't retire?
   a Bill Gates
   b J.K. Rowling
   c Fidel Castro

5 (**3.8**) Complete the words. Listen and check.

1 **A** Who sent you that letter?
   B I r_____ d__'_ k___. I've got no i___ !

2 **A** Do you know the actress Rebecca Hall?
   B Who? No. I've never h_____ of h__!

3 **A** Who recorded the album *Circus*?
   B I'm n___ s____ . Can you give me a c____ ?

4 **A** Who sang *Hung Up*?
   B That's an e____ o__ . Every_____ k_____ that. It was M_____.

5 **A** Who discovered Uranium?
   B Uranium? T____'_ a t_____ one. N__. Y__ t___ m_ .

3F Take a break!

Vocabulary

Word Bank 10: Phrasal verbs p. 73

Nouns: back-packing, career, currency, customer, customs, employee, gap year, health insurance, homepage, niece, qualification, safety, teenager

Adjectives: afraid, certain, glad, individual

Verbs: deal with, earn, fancy, give up, go back, grow up, look after, look for, pay for, pick up, retire, set off, sort out

Test yourself on Unit 3

1 Do these exercises to check your progress.

2 Count your **correct** answers.
Write the total number in the box.

Total: ☐ /40 correct answers

3 Try to understand your mistakes. If necessary,
- read the **Essential Grammar**, and/or
- look at the Student Book lesson again, or
- ask your teacher.

4 How do you feel after this unit? Tick (✓) a box.

👍👍☐ 👍☐ ✊☐ 👎☐ 👎👎☐

I can use phrasal verbs. (Lesson 3F)

1 Circle the correct option.

1 My dad hated sport for years but now he's *made / taken* up golf.

2 I need a babysitter to *look / keep* after the kids.

3 My mother's going to *take / give up* her job and travel round the world.

4 We *looked / found out* some interesting information on the Net.

5 I *picked / put* up some useful skills on that course.

6 We threw *away / up* a lot of rubbish today. Our flat looks much better.

2 Tick (✓) the correct sentences. Correct the wrong ones.

1 ☐ Her children are growing up quickly.

2 ☐ Are you good at dealing with customers?

3 ☐ My wife's gone to university back.

4 ☐ I'm looking a pencil for.

5 ☐ Take your coat off and come into the kitchen.

6 ☐ She clicked the icon on.

7 ☐ Our kids usually stay late up at the weekend.

8 ☐ My father paid our dinner for.

I can use must *and* have to. (Lesson 3A)

3 Read the information. Then write sentences with *must, mustn't, have to* or *don't have to* and the verb in **bold**.

1 You cannot **leave** work before 5 p.m.

You mustn't leave work before 5 p.m..

2 You can **wear** a tie if you want to. It's your choice.

_____

3 Everybody **has** an identity card. It's the law.

_____

4 This is secret information. Don't **show** it to anybody.

_____

5 The school provides lunch but you can **eat** it at home if you prefer.

_____

I can use the Present perfect to connect the past and the present. (Lesson 3B)

4 Complete with *for* or *since*.

1 My uncle has lived in Italy _____ the 1970s.

2 Your photo has been on my website _____ five months.

3 Cheri's worked for BMW _____ a long time.

4 We've had no letters _____ Monday.

5 I haven't seen my sister _____ my birthday party.

6 They haven't gone on holiday _____ five years!

5 Add one of these words to each sentence.

| a | anything | of | nobody | somebody |
| | something | somewhere | which |

1 Hot is the opposite *of* cold.

2 An atlas is book that has lots of maps.

3 A DJ is who plays music in a nightclub.

4 A library is you can borrow books.

5 A squid is an animal looks like an octopus.

6 A frying pan is that you use for cooking.

7 It's illegal to enter the club after 2 a.m. can go in.

8 It's midnight and there's no electricity. I can't see at all.

6 Read the information. Compare the apartments using *as ... as* and the adjectives.

Apartment	A1	A2	A3
Size	75m²	80m²	80m²
Price to rent	€900 a month	€800 a month	€900 a month
Built	2009	1960	1992
Distance from centre	1km	2km	2km
Condition	almost new	very dirty	very clean
Neighbours	very noisy	quiet	quiet

1 A2 *is as large as* A3.
   (large)

2 A1 _____ A3.
   (expensive)

3 A2 _____ A1.
   (modern)

4 A3 _____ A2.
   (close to the centre)

5 A2 _____ A1.
   (clean)

6 The neighbours in A3 _____ the neighbours in A1.
   (noisy)

7 (3.0) Write subject questions and add words (✳). Listen and check.

1 who / star / ✳ *The Dark Knight*?
   A: *Who starred in The Dark Knight?*
   B: It was Christian Bale ... and, um, Heath Ledger.

2 who / live ✳ 10 Downing Street?
   A: _____
   B: That's the official home of the British Prime Minister.

3 who / paint / *Guernica* ✳ 1937?
   A: _____
   B: Pablo Picasso. It's my favourite painting.

4 which / city / host ✳ Olympic Games ✳ 2008?
   A: _____
   B: If I remember rightly, it was Beijing.

5 which team / win ✳ football World Cup ✳ 2006?
   A: _____
   B: Italy, 5−3 on penalties against France.

6 who / record ✳ album *Favourite Worst Nightmare* ✳ 2007?
   A: _____
   B: That's easy. It was the Arctic Monkeys. It's great.

8 Cover the words and test yourself on ...

1 (WB) Verbs, adjectives and prepositions (p.71)
Can you remember the 10 phrases?

2 (WB) Driving (p.72)
Can you pronounce the 9 places on the map?
Can you remember the 12 prepositions of movement?

3 (WB) Phrasal verbs (p.73)
Can you remember the 20 phrasal verbs?

4 (Phrasebook 3) (p.78) Look only at your translations.
Can you remember the phrases in English?

4A Memorable moments

1 Complete the adjectives.

1 Our daughter is the first person in our family to go to college. We're so p_ _ _ _ _ of her.

2 The doctor told me to stay in bed because I felt s_ _ _ _ .

3 I think my sister's j_ _ _ _ _ _ _ of me because I have a better car, a bigger house, and a better job!

4 Are you i_ _ _ _ _ _ _ _ _ _ in Modern Art? I've got a really good book on it that I can lend you.

5 Lisa's really u_ _ _ _ _ because her cat's died.

6 I said 'congratulations' to Claudia, but she isn't pregnant – Mel is! I was so e_ _ _ _ _ _ _ _ _ _ _ .

2 Rewrite two sentences into one with *-ing* as the subject.

1 I hate working in an office. It's really boring.
   Working in an office is really boring.

2 I travel to work on the train and it's very expensive.
   _____

3 You should go swimming. It's great for your health.
   _____

4 Don't eat a lot of sugar. It's bad for your teeth.
   _____

5 I love playing football. It's brilliant!
   _____

6 I want to learn English but it's really difficult.
   _____

7 We text a lot. They're a lot cheaper than calling.
   _____

3 (4.1) Complete with these phrases.

> didn't feel like going   didn't mind living
> enjoyed being   finished packing
> gave up working   remember having
> suggested working

My last day of school was a special day for me. I was a bit upset to leave because I (1) _____ at school. I had really good teachers and lots of friends. But that day was important for me because I (2) _____ a really important conversation with my teacher, Mrs Terry.

I was in the classroom and just as I (3) _____ my bag, she came in to say 'goodbye'. Before she left, she asked me about my future plans. I told her I didn't know what to do. I (4) _____ to university because I wanted to go travelling first. She listened to me and then she (5) _____ as a volunteer in the developing world. She said it was a great experience if I (6) _____ in a place without water, electricity and things like that. At that time, I had a summer job in a supermarket but after our conversation, I (7) _____ there and went to India to help teach children at a local school. I'm really proud of the work I did there.

4 Write sentences using a preposition and *-ing*.

1 Tony ✻ angry ✻ lose ✻ his watch
   Tony's angry about losing his watch.

2 Alexander Fleming ✻ famous ✻ discover penicillin
   _____

3 we ✻ worried ✻ fail ✻ Maths exam
   _____

4 I ✻ bored ✻ do ✻ such ✻ lot ✻ revision
   _____

5 dad ✻ really ✻ bad ✻ cooking
   _____

6 Vicki ✻ study ✻ tomorrow's test ✻ tired
   _____

7 kids ✻ excited ✻ go ✻ holiday tomorrow
   _____

8 I ✻ interested ✻ hear ✻ your
   _____

Looking good

Vocabulary

Word Bank 7: Useful verbs p. 70   **Nouns:** advert, cosmetic surgery, diet, lady, lemon, muscle, weight
Adjectives: believable, careful, healthy, obese   **Verbs:** advertise, apply, promise, regret, serve
Expressions: Right then. Anyway.

1 Correct the mistakes.

           will
1 ***He shall go the gym this evening.***

2 ***My mother may to have an operation.***

3 I not might go to the beauty salon tonight.

4 They wont see you without an appointment.

5 If you will go to the gym, I'll meet you in the cafe.

6 ***My sister might to lend you some face cream. Ask her.***

7 *I'm really late. Shall you help me pack, please?*

2 Circle the correct option.

1 **A:** Is Rocco coming to football tomorrow?

  B: I'm not sure. He hurt his foot last week so he
    (1) *might not / won't* play.

2 **A:** Maybe we could have steak tomorrow?

  B: No, Suzie's a vegetarian. She (2) *might not / won't* eat it.

3 **A:** Have you seen the weather report?

  B: Yeah. They said (3) *it might / it'll* rain. It's 50-50.

4 **A:** I haven't put on any sun cream. I don't need it.

  B: It's 38° and really sunny! With your white skin (4) *you might / you'll* regret it.

5 **A:** Frank wants to stay in a five star hotel when we're in Tokyo.

  B: (5) *It might / It'll* cost you a lot of money.

6 **A:** My cousin's coming to England with us but she can't speak any English!

  B: She (6) *might not / won't* understand anything.

7 **A:** Bob looks like a model. All the girls love him.

  B: I'm sure he *might / 'll* be the most popular boy at the party.

3 (4.2) Listen. Tick (✓) the sentence you hear.

1 a We won't see you tomorrow. ☐
  b We want to see you tomorrow. ☐

2 a They won't go on a diet. ☐
  b They want to go on a diet. ☐

3 a You won't be here tomorrow. ☐
  b You want to be here tomorrow. ☐

4 a I won't get a coffee. ☐
  b I want to get a coffee. ☐

4 (4.3) Paul's pessimistic. He always thinks bad things will happen. Olivia's the opposite, an optimist. They're arranging a party. Complete with *will*, *won't* or *might* and the verbs. Listen and check.

Olivia: We've invited 20 people to the party so we (1) _____ (have) lots of guests tomorrow.

Paul: I don't think anybody (2) _____ (come). There's a big football match tomorrow and everybody (3) _____ (stay) at home and watch it on TV.

Olivia: They (4) _____ (do) that! All the girls told me they're coming to the party.

Paul: Well, we (5) _____ (see) tomorrow. Anyway, we should go to the supermarket today because it (6) _____ (not / have) all the food we want tomorrow.

Olivia: But we don't need to buy lots of food because everyone (7) _____ (bring) something to eat.

Paul: My friends (8) _____ (bring) anything so I think we should buy a lot of food.

Olivia: Right, then let's get a lot. We (9) _____ (buy) too much but I think it (10) _____ (be) OK.

4C Friends for life?

1 Circle the correct preposition.

1 I was great friends with Cath at school but I've lost touch *of / with / to* her now.

2 Every time I eat olives, I think *on / for / of* my first holiday in Turkey.

3 The teacher shouted *at / to / on* me because I didn't do the homework.

4 You need to fill *on / in / over* the online application form.

5 What happened *to / at / on* you? You're over two hours late!

6 I'm going to ask Gary *by / for / to* some help.

7 Have you listened *at / to / by* the new CD yet?

8 My friend wants to go to a Razorlight concert but I've never heard *over / for / of* them!

2 Match problems 1–6 to the advice, a–f. There's one extra.

1 I've lost touch with so many old friends. It's sad.

2 I'm really worried about cooking for five guests.

3 That new supermarket is much too expensive.

4 I've got loads of books and I don't need any of them.

5 I'm in love with Daniela but she doesn't know.

6 Hurry up! The train leaves in five minutes!

7 I'm really, really tired. More than ever.

a ☐ If you advertise them online, you'll be able to sell them.

b ☐ If you ask them to help with the cooking, they won't complain about the food.

c ☐ If you leave now, you'll catch it.

d ☐ If you go to bed for half an hour, you'll feel better.

e ☐ If you buy your fruit and vegetables in the market, you'll save some money.

f ☐ If you tell her, she might go out with you.

3 Complete with *will*, *won't*, *might*, *the* or *some* and another word.

1 Nina ___*might*___ come to ___*the*___ party if you invite her and ___*some*___ of her friends.

2 If you give _____ your email address, I'll send you _____ photos of my cat.

3 Mr Smith definitely _____ help us if we don't ask him. But, if we ask him nicely, he _____.

4 If they don't _____ any revision, they _____ pass _____ exam.

5 Grandma _____ be really pleased if you get her _____ flowers.

6 I _____ give Yasser _____ message when I see him.

4 Correct the two mistakes in each sentence.

1 *If weather's nice this afternoon, we go to the beach.*

2 *Do you keep a secret, if I telling you something?*

3 *We don't will get to the airport on time, if there will be a lot of cars on the road.*

4 ***If you ate all those chocolates, you don't eat your dinner.***

5 *I get some milk today if I going to the shops.*

6 *If you tell to the teacher the truth, you will have any problems.*

5 **(4.4)** Order the dialogue, 1–11. Listen and check.

a ☐ You're right. They will. When do they get home?

b ☐ OK, that's seven hours. If we start cleaning now, we'll finish before they come back.

c ☐ At the door? Who is it?

d ☐1 Spiros, look at your house! That party was a bit too crazy.

e ☐ No, we won't! We'll never finish in time. There's too much to do!

f ☐ OK. Where's their number?

g ☐ Crazy! This is a disaster. If my parents see this, they'll kill me.

h ☐ Well, if we phone Jackie and Elena, they'll come over and help us.

i ☐ 5 o'clock – today!

j ☐ You don't want to know...

k ☐ I'll get it. There's someone at the door.

I earn too much!

Vocabulary

Word Bank 5: Adjectives p. 68
Nouns: alphabet, camping, hypermarket, position, promotion, supermarket
Adjectives: complimentary, efficient, fair, intuitive, self-critical, unfriendly   **Verb:** laugh

1 Find 12 adjectives.

M	P	O	L	I	T	E	H	I	O	S	Q
F	E	X	P	E	R	I	E	N	C	E	D
R	L	F	S	H	Y	K	T	T	R	L	A
I	N	T	U	I	T	I	V	E	U	F	G
T	B	H	L	A	Z	Y	S	L	D	C	G
L	L	Q	M	G	E	N	T	L	E	A	R
M	E	N	E	R	G	E	T	I	C	L	E
T	S	F	C	H	K	W	D	G	E	M	S
Y	Q	U	A	L	I	F	I	E	D	I	S
F	Y	D	L	Y	B	Q	J	N	O	C	I
Y	Z	H	M	Q	U	I	E	T	F	A	V
U	N	F	R	I	E	N	D	L	Y	L	E

2 Add one of these words to each sentence.

> a   faster   little   much   more   than

1 My new boss is a /more organised than my last one. *little*
2 I earn much money than you.
3 Zelda is quicker worker than me.
4 Joe's a bit on the computer than me.
5 My girlfriend gets paid a lot more money me.
6 It's easier to fly around Latin America than drive.

3 Two options (a–c) can complete the sentence. Cross out the incorrect option.

1 Katie works _____ more hours than Dino.
   a ~~lot~~   **b** a lot   **c** loads
2 We have _____ more time than you.
   a a little   **b** bit   **c** a lot
3 Vijay earns _____ more money than me.
   a a bit   **b** much   **c** many
4 You're _____ than us.
   a more experienced   **b** faster   **c** most efficient
5 Alfredo's _____ more hard working than Heinrich.
   a a little   **b** some   **c** a bit

4 (4.5) Listen. Underline the most stressed word in B's responses.

1 **A:** I don't earn enough money.
   B: What? You earn <u>much</u> more than me!

2 A: Do you want to work with Enzo or Paula?
   B: Paula. She's a little more organised than Enzo.

3 A: Shall we go to Seville or Edinburgh?
   B: Well, Spain's much hotter than Scotland at the moment.

4 A: You don't look very optimistic.
   B: No, because this year's going to be much worse than last year.

5 A: Do you like your job?
   B: Yeah. My new company's much better than my old one.

6 A: Bus or taxi? We haven't got much time, you know.
   B: The taxi's a lot more expensive.

7 A: The office workers start work at 9 a.m.
   B: Well, I start much earlier than them. I'm here at 5!

5 Read the poem. Do you agree with this?

> ### Why I hate studying
>
> The more we study, the less we know.
> The more we know, the more we forget.
> The more we forget, the less we know.
> The less we know, the less we forget.
> The less we forget, the more we know.
> So? Why study?

Study tip

Learning English spelling isn't easy. After the teacher corrects your homework, list the words that you spelt wrongly. Try to use some of them next time you write. When you're sure how to spell a word, cross it off your list.

4E Changes

Vocabulary

Word Bank 12: Vowel and consonant sounds p. 75
Nouns: accent, fresh air, block of apartments, couple, drama, flat, gardener, lawyer, neighbour
Adjectives: dramatic, lovely, personal, polluted, retired, stressful   **Verbs:** commute, encourage
Expressions: The good old days. How do you do? Are you all right? What's up?

1 Find and correct 11 more mistakes.

> *going*
> I enjoyed ~~to go~~ to university. I didn't mind have
> to spend a long time reading old books or study
> websites on the Internet. I remember stay up all
> night, night after night just before take my exams.
> I didn't sleep much but it didn't stop me from go
> to parties all weekend. I wanted to go on study and
> to do an MA too but live at a university was too
> expensive and I decided leave and get a job. One
> day I really hope go back and I would love to finish
> doing my MA and perhaps even go on study and do a
> PhD. I really want to becoming a professor.

2 Circle the correct option.

1 We *use / used* to cycle to school.

2 Did you *use / used* to have long hair?

3 My family didn't *use / used* to eat a lot of fish.

4 My granddad *use / used* to have a dog called Rocky.

5 Didn't you *use / used* to live next to the station?

6 When she was a child, Carol didn't *use / used* to eat vegetables at all.

3 Read the information. Complete the responses.

1 **A:** I didn't like coffee when I was a child.
   B: You mean *you didn't use to like coffee* .

2 **A:** My kids played basketball a lot at school.
   B: You mean _____ .

3 **A:** They didn't have a computer ten years ago.
   B: You mean _____ .

4 **A:** Luca always stayed with his grandparents during the school holidays.
   B: You mean _____ .

5 **A:** As a boy, I often went walking in the hills.
   B: You mean _____ .

6 **A:** In the past, this café didn't serve hot meals.
   B: You mean _____ .

4 Complete with *used to* and these verbs.

> be   give   make   not eat
> not show   speak   take   wear

The Good Old Days

The 1970s is only thirty years ago but life (1)_____ very different. For example, nowadays, parents buy designer clothes for their children, but my mother (2)_____ clothes for me and my brother. TV was better but there were only three channels in the UK and they (3)_____ any TV programmes in the mornings!

School was different too. We had a school uniform and we (4)_____ short trousers even in winter! It was stricter too. For example, only the teachers (5)_____ in class: we didn't say anything. And homework (6)_____ ages to do because there was no Internet or anything like that. The food was terrible. I (7)_____ anything at the school canteen because it was so disgusting and the teachers (8)_____ me punishments because I refused to eat the food.

5 (4.6) Do the quiz. Listen and check. Which questions did Nicolo get right?

> **1 Which country used to be called Siam?**
>   **a** Burma **b** Vietnam **c** Thailand
>
> **2 What did English people use to say when they met someone new?**
>   **a** How do you do? **b** Are you OK?
>   **c** What's up?
>
> **3 Which football team did David Beckham use to play for?**
>   **a** Arsenal **b** Bayern Munich **c** Real Madrid
>
> **4 Which city used to be the capital of Australia?**
>   **a** Melbourne **b** Perth **c** Darwin
>
> **5 Which American politician used to live in Indonesia?**
>   **a** Bill Clinton **b** Barak Obama **c** Al Gore

Keeping a record

Vocabulary

Word Bank 12: Vowel and consonant sounds p. 75   **Word Bank 2:** The verb *get* p. 65

Word Bank 11: More verbs and prepositions p. 74

Nouns: album, chat, code, diarist, diary, feedback, festival, future generations, podcast, videocam

Adjectives: electronic, end-of-course, fascinating, historical, horrible   **Adverbs:** immediately, otherwise

Expressions: Do you want anything? That's nice. How is Chris, by the way?

Test yourself on Unit 4

1 Do these exercises to check your progress.

2 Count your **correct** answers.
Write the total number in the box.

Total: ☐ /40 correct answers

3 Try to understand your mistakes. If necessary,
- read the **Essential Grammar**, and/or
- look at the Student Book lesson again, or
- ask your teacher.

4 How do you feel after this unit? Tick (✓) a box.

👍👍☐   👍☐   ✋☐   👎☐   👎👎☐

I can use verb tenses. (Lessons 4A–4F)

1 Complete with the correct verb forms.

Claire: I (1) *'m going* (go) to town this afternoon.
Do you want anything?

Rachel: No. I went this morning. I bought a ring. Look.
I (2) _____ (wear) it now.

Claire: Oh yeah. That's nice.

Rachel: I (3) _____ (never / see) one like it
before, so I had to buy it.

Claire: Where did you get it?

Rachel: I bought it in the jewellery shop while I
(4) _____ (walk) around the shopping
centre with Chris.

Claire: How is Chris by the way? I (5) _____
(see) him recently.

Rachel: He's OK but he's a bit nervous because he's
studying for his exams.

2 Complete with a verb + *back*.

phrase	the opposite direction
1 Come back here.	Go _back there_ .
2 I took the keys.	I _put the keys back_ .
3 She emailed me.	I _____ .
4 I bought a shirt.	I took _____ .
5 We drive to work.	We _____ .
6 Go on the next lesson.	Go _____ .
7 I gave them the money.	They _____ .

I can use the -ing *form.* (Lesson 4A)

3 Circle the correct preposition.

1 My brother's really good *at / in* writing in English.

2 We're proud *of / about* helping poor people.

3 Liz is different *from / with* her sister.

4 Cervantes is famous *of / for* writing *Don Quixote*.

5 Alan's worried *with / about* failing the exam.

I can talk about the future with will *and* might.
(Lesson 4B)

4 Complete with *will*, *won't* or *might* and a verb.

	Tomorrow's weather	Temperature
Mumbai	☁	10–20°C
London	⛅	5–10°C
Tokyo	☀	15–20°C
Rio de Janeiro	⛈	22°C
Stockholm	❄	–5°C

1 It _won't be_ hotter in Mumbai than in Tokyo. *(be)*

2 It _____ in Stockholm. *(snow)*

3 It _____ sunny in London. *(be)*

4 It _____ in Tokyo. *(rain)*

5 They _____ storms in Rio de Janeiro. *(have)*

5 Match the sentence halves and complete.

1 If I change my hair colour,

2 If you go to the gym every day,

3 If you go on the website,

4 They'll give you a job

5 You can't go to work today

6 Your boss will be really angry

a ☐ if you're late _____ work again.

b ☐ if you _____ enthusiastic in the interview.

c ☐ if you _____ ill.

d [1] I 'll_____ go blonde.

e ☐ you'll _____ able to see everyone's comments.

f ☐ you'll _____ weight.

6 Add one more word to each sentence. There's one correct sentence.

       slightly
1 Henry was a ∕ slower worker than me.

2 You're earning loads more money Jürgen.

3 Jorge speaks Spanish much better me.

4 Wendy has been a lot efficient than Jimmy.

5 The red watch is bit more expensive than the blue one.

6 Nicki might be little more experienced than Carlos.

7 I'm slightly more relaxed about this test than last year's.

8 Alex was faster than Elke. He won that race easily.

7 Circle the correct verb forms.

Nelson Rolihlahla Mandela (1) *was born* / *born* on 18th July 1918. He (2) *has been* / *was* President of South Africa from 1994–99. Before that, Mandela (3) *was* / *was being* in prison for 27 years because he (4) *use to* / *used to* be the leader of the African National Congress.

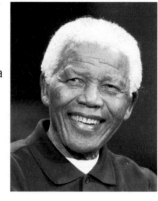

During his 18 years on Robben Island he (5) *didn't used to* / *use to* be allowed to see anybody. When Mandela (6) *left* / *used to leave* prison on 11 February 1990, it (7) *was* / *used to be* on live TV all over the world.

He (8) *won* / *used to win* the Nobel Peace Prize in 1993 and (9) *retired* / *used to retire* from politics in 1999. But until July 2008 he (10) *wasn't going* / *didn't use to* be allowed to enter the USA.

Mandela (11) *got* / *used to get* married three times, (12) *had* / *was having* six children, twenty grandchildren, and lots of great-grandchildren.

8 Cover the words and test yourself on ...

1 **WB** Verbs, adjectives and prepositions (p.71)

Can you remember the 8 phrases?

2 **WB** More verbs and prepositions (p.74)

Can you remember the 24 phrases?

3 **WB** Vowel and consonant sounds (p.75)

Can you pronounce all the words?

4 **WB** Irregular verbs (p.76)

Can you remember all the irregular verbs?

5 **Phrasebook 4** (p.78) Look only at your translations.

Can you remember the phrases in English?

Student book

1.3 1A Exercise 4

Jill: Wow, Sam! You're very brown. How was your holiday?

Sam: Amazing, Jill. We had a wonderful time.

Jill: We? Who did you go with?

Sam: Some old friends from school. They're really into diving and asked me to go with them.

Jill: Lucky you! Why didn't you tell me before? I'd love to go to Egypt!

Sam: Sorry, but, it was a last minute thing and, you know …

Jill: Don't worry. I was really busy last week. So, what was the weather like in Egypt?

Sam: It was boiling. But it didn't matter. We went diving every day and the evenings were beautiful.

Jill: Wow! What were the people like?

Sam: They were lovely. Really friendly.

Jill: Where did you stay?

Sam: In a five star hotel in Sharm El Sheik!

Jill: But wasn't that expensive?

Sam: No, not at all. We got a package holiday and everything was included.

Jill: Nice one. Did you see much of Egypt?

Sam: Not really. We stayed at the hotel most of the time.

Jill: Didn't you want to see the Pyramids?

Sam: Yes, of course, I did. But, we only had a week and there just wasn't time to fly to Cairo.

Jill: And what was the diving like?

Sam: Brilliant. The Red Sea is unbelievable. It's incredibly clean and there were literally millions of fish.

1.4 1A Exercise 8

1

Reporter: With me here is Surya Pandey from Dingboche, a village near Mount Everest where the tour group disappeared yesterday. Surya, what's the weather like there now?

Surya: Oh, it's awful, absolutely awful. It's snowing, freezing cold; it was ten degrees below freezing an hour ago. And the winds are very strong.

Reporter: But why didn't somebody stop the tour group before they left?

Surya: The weather was fine yesterday; just a bit cloudy, that's all. But then suddenly, the weather changed. There were storms and everything. The rescue team tried to find them again this morning but the day ended without any news. It's terrible, and it looks like they aren't …

2

Vanessa: Incredible story this. Tell us more, Marty.

Marty: Right, Vanessa. Well, the fire started two days ago in a forest in southern California. There were really strong winds and the fire grew quickly, very, very fast, and moved towards Topanga. There was a real danger of Topangans losing their homes. The police told everybody to leave but they refused.

Vanessa: So, why didn't they leave?

Marty: Good question. It was really scary. But the people here have really big hearts and, well, nobody wanted to go without a fight. Nobody. Hundreds

of them worked non-stop with the firefighters. They made lines, passing water from hand to hand, all day and all night, until, well, they stopped the fire and saved their homes. Yes, incredible.

1.7 1B Exercise 8

Bess: Hello?

Si: Hi Bess. It's Si.

Bess: Hi there. Is everything OK?

Si: Fine. Look, you know we're having a special 'Environment Day' on 4th June? Well, I'm organising it and I need your help!

Bess: Sure, no problem. How can I help?

Si: Right, well, a lot of important scientists are coming to talk about different things, like pollution and recycling and things. We've got Mark Barnard too! He's giving a lecture on climate change in the morning.

Bess: Wow! That's good!

Si: Yeah. The problem is – he's arriving by train at 8.30. I'm meeting the other speakers at 8.15 so I can't pick him up at the station. Could you do that for me?

Bess: Of course I can. No problem.

Si: You're a star! Look, we're having a meal at Zebedee's at 12.30. Would you like to come with us?

Bess: Zebedee's? How can I say 'no'?

Si: Thanks a million, Bess! Speak soon. Bye!

1.9 1C Exercise 5

Mona: So, Dave, when are you off to 'The Smiling Alligator Hotel'? That is a wonderful name!

Dave: Isn't it? I'm getting the plane tomorrow night. There's going to be a Land Rover waiting for me at the airport.

Mona: How exciting! What an amazing place to visit for work!

Dave: I know. It's going to be brilliant! You and I have incredible jobs, don't we?

Mona: Yeah! I get the south of England and you get South America! Don't forget to write the holiday report!

Dave: Don't worry. I'm going to write about everything I do.

Mona: We'll see!

Dave: I've got it all planned. I'm going to spend the first day by the pool. I'm not going to do anything, just swim, sleep and use the sauna. Oh, and write my report in the evening.

Mona: What else are you going to do?

Dave: Well. I'm going to go fishing and go for long walks in the rainforest. And, you know what, I think I'll try to use the hotel gym too.

Mona: Really? You in the gym! Well, I can't wait to read your report in next month's magazine! And think of me back here, getting cold and wet in the rain!

Dave: Don't worry. I will.

1.13 1D Exercise 2

Interviewer: And now we have Phil on the line. So / Phil – / tell us about your terrible journey. Where were you going?

Phil: Hi Jane. / Well, / last week / I had a meeting in Cardiff / and I decided to take the train. / I don't like travelling to Cardiff by car / because of the traffic.

Interviewer: Yes, / it can be awful!

Phil: Well, / when I woke up / it was pouring with rain / and the radio said there were loads of problems on the roads. / So, / I checked online about the trains / and it seemed the trains were working fine. / But / my taxi journey to the station was terrible. / There were floods on some of the roads / and the 15 minute journey took over an hour!

Interviewer: Oh no!

Phil: Right! / And when I walked into the station, / I couldn't believe it. / It was full of people. / Some were standing, / others were sitting on their bags. / Loads were queuing for tickets / and some were even waiting outside in the rain! / And there weren't any trains. / They were all cancelled!

Interviewer: Wonderful!

Phil: Yes! / So, we waited / for another hour! / Finally, / a bus came / and took us slowly to the next station.

Interviewer: Oh, yuk.

Phil: Yes, / and there, / of course, / more cold, / tired people were waiting on the platforms. / When the train came it was really crowded. / People were standing / and / babies were crying. / One child got travel sick. / Everybody was having a horrible time. / The air in the carriages was hot / and wet. / It was an awful journey.

Interviewer: I can imagine.

Phil: We got to Cardiff nearly three hours late. / It was still raining.

Interviewer: Of course!

Phil: And I wasn't feeling very well. / I was tired, / hungry, / angry, / late for my meeting / and I got completely wet because I left my umbrella on the train! / Next time / I'm going to drive!

Interviewer: I don't blame you!

1.18 1F Exercise 2

Ana: Do you like going to new places on holiday or going back to places that you know?

Bob: That's an easy question! We always go somewhere new. It's good to see different countries, do different things and meet different people. How about you?

Ana: Oh, the same as you. But it isn't always easy to choose where to go.

Bob: So, how do you choose a new place?

Ana: Well, usually, we get ideas from our friends. People talk about their holidays – where they went, what it was like – you know, and sometimes I think 'Yeah, I'd like to go there.' People who know a place can give you ideas about where to stay, where to go, where not to go!

1.19 1F Exercise 3

Ana: People who know a place can give you ideas about where to stay, where to go, where not to go!

Bob: Very true!

Ana: So, how about you? Last year you went to Scotland, didn't you? Why did you go there?

Bob: Well – you'll think this is strange but Beth and I go on 'Location Vacations'!

Ana: What on earth's a 'Location Vacation'?
Bob: It's getting really popular these days. It's when you visit places from films.
Ana: Right! You see a film and you think you'd like to really visit the place they made the film in?
Bob: Yeah. So Scotland was part of the 'Da Vinci Code holiday tour'.
Ana: Of course! That little church in Scotland where they went at the end?
Bob: Yes. We also went to the cathedral they used and lots of other different places. It was fantastic.
Ana: What a good idea. Where are you going next year?
Bob: Not sure yet. We'll have to see what's on at the cinema next month!

1.21 Revision 1 Exercise 6

Brad: It happened on Friday night.
Vicky: Right.
Brad: I was going out with my girlfriend for a meal and to watch a movie. We decided to get the subway downtown like we always do. Anyway, when we got to the subway, there was an old man and he was sitting in the street.
Vicky: How old was he?
Brad: About seventy years old and he had blood on his face and he didn't look well.
Vicky: That's strange.
Brad: Yeah. So, I asked if he was OK. He just said he was shopping.
Vicky: Shopping?
Brad: He was buying some candy for his grandkids. But really he wasn't doing anything. He was not OK. Maybe he fell over or something.
Vicky: What did you do?
Brad: Well, I was worried about him so I called an ambulance on my cell phone. Luckily, they came in ten minutes and they took him to hospital. So, I hope he's OK now.

2.8 2C Exercise 6

A: A lot of applications. That's good.
B: OK. So, who have we got?
A: Well, I really like Brad. He's gorgeous!
B: He's not bad I suppose.
A: He's not too old for the show and he's quite intelligent. What do you think?
B: But is he energetic enough? It says here he likes reading and watching TV. A bit boring?
A: Yeah, you're right.
B: OK. So, who else is there?
A: There's Laura. She's really energetic. She's always doing Exercise or sports.
B: But look, she says she never gets angry! I think she's a bit too calm.
A: No, that's no good. Ok, so Laura's out.
B: Anyone else you like?
A: There is one possibility. It's Angie. I know she's 55 but that's not too old. She's friendly, she's certainly not too shy, very funny and she has some strong opinions.
B: I'm not sure. I don't think she's interesting enough for the show.
A: But have you read her CV? She has some very unusual hobbies.
B: OK, OK, you win. We'll have her.

2.13 2D Exercise 8

Rosa: No, I don't think I'm like any of these people. I don't think about computers all the time. I just bought the cheapest laptop I could find and I use it normally.

Marco: Ah! But what is normal for you? And yes, I know you got the cheapest computer but I'm sure you don't like it when it's a bit slow.
Rosa: OK. I'd like it to be a bit faster. But that doesn't mean I'm a geek or an addict or compulsive!
Marco: True. I'm the same. I just use mine for research, sending e-mails, chatting a bit.
Rosa: And buying things!
Marco: OK. Shopping too!

2.14 2D Exercise 9

Marco: But my brother – I mean, he's one of those compulsive gamers. In fact, he's the most compulsive one I know. He lives for computer games!
Rosa: Really?
Marco: Yes. He's got the best laptop in the family and no one else is allowed to touch it! He spends all his money on that computer.
Rosa: I bet he's good at games too?
Marco: Oh yeah. He's the cleverest gamer in the school. He won a really big competition last weekend.
Rosa: Wow!
Marco: And this article is right. He's also a hardware addict. He wants to have the most recent technology for his games.
Rosa: Do you know any hackers? They must be really clever.
Marco: No, no hackers. But I do know a Computer Immigrant. My grandad! He's just the slowest learner! He's always asking me how to send e-mails.

2.15 2E Exercise 5

Reporter: Today I'm talking to Mike Rogers who came to help here in Kenya eighteen months ago. We are at an elephant orphanage. Mike, can you tell us a little about the work you do here?
Mike: Sure. Here we take care of baby elephants that have lost their parents.
Reporter: By that, you mean, that their parents have died?
Mike: Yes. Perhaps they've died from natural causes or perhaps hunters have killed them. Without a parent, the baby elephants will die. They need somebody to look after them.
Reporter: And you bring them here.
Mike: Yes. Sometimes they're very young – a few days or weeks. We look after them and keep them safe.
Reporter: Do they stay here for the rest of their lives?

2.16 2E Exercise 6

Mike: Oh, no. They only stay until they are ready to go back to the wild.
Reporter: Since you arrived, have you saved many elephants?
Mike: Yes. We've saved a lot. Unfortunately we've lost a couple too. They were too young to help.
Reporter: Oh dear. But, generally, are you happy to be here?
Mike: To be honest – this is the most rewarding thing I have ever done. I love the country, the people and I love helping the animals. It's the first time I've been to Africa and it's the most beautiful country in the world!

Reporter: I imagine it's the most difficult job you have ever done too!
Mike: Yes. The most difficult thing is when we lose an elephant. I cry quite a lot then. But I am so glad I came. It's the best decision I've ever made.

2.22 2F Exercise 7

Carol: Hi Tom. Tell us what's happening downtown.
Tom: Well Carol, the streets are absolutely full of people! It's so crowded we had to leave our car and walk.
Carol: Really? What's up?
Tom: Yeah. Well, they're demonstrating against plans for a new hypermarket.
Carol: A what?
Tom: You know, they're going to build this enormous supermarket next to the river. It's such a beautiful green area ...
Carol: Ah, I see ...
Tom: Right, and everybody here is so unhappy. Many of them are getting really angry.
Carol: I can imagine.
Tom: Anyway, it's such a big demonstration that they've closed the town centre completely.
Carol: Is there any sign of trouble?
Tom: No, not at all. It's been 100% peaceful. People are angry and shouting, but the organizers insisted there should be no violence and, well, so far, so good.

2.24 Revision 2 Exercise 6

Carl: I went to see that new film last night, *The Watchmen*.
Nicola: Oh yeah. Who did you go with?
Carl: Well, that was the problem. The film's about superheroes, right? So, I thought it was for kids. And me and my brother wanted to go, but the film is an 18!
Nicola: And your brother's only about 15, isn't he?
Carl: Exactly! He's too young to see it at the cinema. He couldn't go. So, I went with my friend Jim instead.
Nicola: Did you enjoy it?
Carl: Yeah, I did. Have you seen it?
Nicola: Yeah, I have. I liked it.
Carl: But?
Nicola: It was a bit too violent for me: there was too much fighting and action.
Carl: It's always like that in the movies. I thought it was good. I've read the comic and I think that was better, because there are more ideas in the comic.
Nicola: Right.
Carl: The movie isn't long enough to include everything from the comic. It's about 400 pages long!
Nicola: Really? I haven't read the comic. I thought some scenes were a bit stupid. There's this blue man who becomes really tall and then travels into space. It's not very realistic, is it?
Carl: It's science fiction! It doesn't need to be realistic!

3.4 3B Exercise 3

Interviewer: Beatriz, you're living in Italy, but you weren't born here, were you?
Beatriz: No, I was born in Mexico.
Interviewer: And is your husband Mexican too?
Beatriz: No, Danny's American. We met in Mexico when I was a student, about seven years ago.

Interviewer: And how long have you been married?

Beatriz: Three, no, four, no, five. Yes, it's been five years now. Wow, time flies! And we have two lovely children.

Interviewer: Lucky you! How long have you been in Italy?

Beatriz: We came here, wow, one, two, three years ago. Sorry, I'm not very good at maths. Yeah, we've been here for three years.

Interviewer: Why did you move here? Did you want to live in another country?

Beatriz: No, I adore Mexico! It was because of my husband's job. He's a designer. But, you know, now I don't want to leave. No way. We love it here!

Interviewer: Do you have a job here too?

Beatriz: Yes. I've worked for a clothing company for six months. It's fun! I'm in love with Italian clothes.

3.5 | 3B Exercise 4

Interviewer: So, now you live_in Florence. Do you like_it here?

Beatriz: Well, we haven't lived here_all the time. We lived_in Rome for the first year. And that was very noisy!

Interviewer: Yes_it's such_a big, busy capital. Life must be easier_in Florence.

Beatriz: Oh yes, it's lovely. We both love_art too, so_it's_a great place to be.

Interviewer: Have you had a lot_of problems since you've been here?

Beatriz: No, we haven't. Well, not_a lot. But the culture's very different to Mexico.

Interviewer: Have you had problems picking_up the language?

Beatriz: Some. It's_a very musical language. It's_easier for me than Danny, because_it's like Spanish. But we both speak_it quite well now!

Interviewer: I see, and what_about the cost of living?

Beatriz: Well, yes. Things_are_a lot more_expensive here than back home. Food, gas, oh sorry, I think you say 'petrol' and, you know, housing, clothes ....

Interviewer: And the good points?

Beatriz: Oh, there_are so many! Italy's_a beautiful country, the food_is amazing, and the coffee, the ice-cream, ...!

Interviewer: OK, OK, now you're making me jealous! So, you've_enjoyed the experience so far?

Beatriz: Of course_and we want to stay here as long as possible. We have a house, jobs and our children go to school here. We_are Italian now!

3.8 | 3C Exercise 7

Sven: Hi Karin. You got a phone message from Johnny.

Karin: Oh yes? What did he say?

Sven: Who's Johnny?

Karin: Oh, Johnny's the guy who sold me my new bike.

Sven: Really? He said that you should meet him at The Rock.

Karin: OK.

Sven: Where's The Rock?

Karin: It's in the city centre. It's a new café which has opened in the High Street.

Sven: I see. He also said you should remember 'Password'.

Karin: Fine.

Sven: What's 'Password'?

Karin: 'Password' is a new game that I got last week. We're going to play it. And I'm now going to have a coffee – coffee is a hot liquid that you drink – and watch some TV – TV is a big box which shows films! OK? Any more questions?

3.14 | 3D Exercise 8

Jenna: Careful Nick! Now, take the next exit off the motorway. It's Junction 5.

Nick: Yeah. I see it. OK. We're coming up to a roundabout. Hey, look at that statue on the roundabout! Who do you think it is?

Jenna: Just watch the road please! Now, at the roundabout take the first exit.

Nick: OK. Now what?

Jenna: Go down the hill and turn right at the crossroads.

Nick: This is a nice little town!

Jenna: Concentrate! We're trying to win this. Go along the road and under the bridge.

Nick: Are we nearly there?

Jenna: Not far. Now, there's a bank on the left. Can you see it?

Nick: Yep. Nice flowers outside.

Jenna: Nick! Just watch the road! Turn left at the bank. Then it's the second turning on the left.

Nick: One, two, three, how many did you say? Oops! Sorry. You can turn round in these main roads, can't you? OK, here we are.

Jenna: And there's the hotel on the right!! Yep, I think we're first!

3.16 | 3E Exercise 3

A: Have you seen this list? It's amazing. Guess who's number 1?

B: Huh? I've got no idea. Could you give me a clue?

A: The King of rock 'n' roll. Ladies and gentlemen, please welcome ...

B: Elvis Presley! Of course! I loved 'Heartbreak Hotel'.

A: Yeah, me too. Anyway Elvis died in 1977 but he's still earning millions of dollars every year. Last year he earned 53 million!

B: Wow! Who else is on the list?

A: Well, there's Kurt Kobain.

B: What did he earn?

A: He earned 50 million dollars.

B: Wow!

A: Then there's John Lennon, you know, the ex-Beatle. He died in 1980!

B: That was ages ago!

A: Right. Wow. The Peanuts guy, Schultz, is next on the list. I love his cartoons. And then there's Einstein.

B: But that's impossible. He was a scientist! Why's he on the list?

A: Yes, but now you can buy special toys and videos for young kids. They're called 'Little Einsteins'! They make a lot of money! He earned 18 million!

B: No way. Who do you think gets all that cash?

A: How should I know? Anyway, then there's the painter, Andy Warhol. And Johnny Cash is on the list too.

B: Never heard of him.

A: No? He had a great voice. Because your mine, I walk the line. Remember?

B: No.

A: Well, he died in 2003. But the film of his life made millions. And number ten is Marilyn Monroe.

B: Still? Well, somebody must be very happy about that.

A: OK. So how long do you think Elvis will stay top of the list?

B: Who knows? Probably forever!

A: And what about today? Which celebrities will make the most money after they die?

B: That's a tricky one. Maybe Madonna? What do you think?

3.19 | 3F Exercise 9

Interviewer: So, Jack, you've decided to give up work?

Jack: Well, yes, just for a year! I'm 50 now and it's time I saw a bit of the world!

Interviewer: And where do you want to go?

Jack: There are so many places I haven't seen. But I've decided to go to Asia first.

Interviewer: What would you like to do there?

Jack: Well, I'd like to travel through lots of different countries. Maybe get work in different places to earn some money.

Interviewer: And how are you planning to travel?

Jack: Oh, I want to use different forms of transport. You know, buses, trains, hire a car maybe. Flying costs too much and you don't really see the country, do you?

Interviewer: And do you need to do much before you set off?

Jack: Oh, not really. I must find out about health insurance and places to stay. And the weather in each place. Oh, and pack too!

Interviewer: And have a goodbye party, of course!

Jack: Of course! I can't wait!

Interviewer: Well, good luck, Jack. Have a great trip!

Jack: Thanks a lot.

3.21 | Revision 3 Exercise 10

Bob: These aren't easy questions, are they?

Ilda: They're easy for me!

Bob: Yes, but you're from Lisbon, Ilda. Anyway, you can test me.

Ilda: OK, first question. What happened in Lisbon on November 1, 1755?

Bob: There was an earthquake. A.

Ilda: Yes! So, you know some answers!

Bob: I studied that at school.

Ilda: Number 2. Here are two famous British writers. Whose family originally came from Portugal?

Bob: I think maybe B. Harold Pinter.

Ilda: Why?

Bob: Because Pinter is an unusual name in the UK.

Ilda: You're right. His family was originally called "da Pinta". That's a very Portuguese name.

Bob: I've got two correct so far!

Ilda: How many people live in Portugal today?

Bob: I don't know. 6 million?

Ilda: Wrong! It's B. About 11 million.

Bob: And number 4? I know this one. Which Portuguese football team won the Champions League in 2004?

Ilda: Sporting?

Bob: It's FC Porto.

Ilda: I hate football. Well, do you know question 5? Much more important. One of the most famous people in Portuguese history.

Bob: Oh, I'm not sure. Vasco da Gama?

Ilda: Your Portuguese pronunciation is terrible, Bob! No, it wasn't Vasco da Gama. It was answer A. Ferdinand Magellan.

Bob: So, I got three out of five. I wonder if anybody got all the answers right?

4.4 4B Exercise 2

A

Is your skin looking tired? Can you see lines around your eyes and mouth? It's time to use our latest cream *Five Star*. We know there are hundreds of creams on the market but *Five Star* is really amazing! Use *Five Star* every morning and night for three months and those lines will go! Your skin will look fresh again and you will definitely look years younger! And with *Five Star Gold*, your skin can also be golden without going to the beach! So what are you waiting for? Go on! Try it! You won't be disappointed. At only $80, *Five Star* will be the best skin cream you ever buy. Promise!

B

Nobody is completely happy with their body. Here at the New Age Cosmetic Hospital we really understand this and are sure we can help you. We have over forty years' experience in cosmetic surgery and are experts in every type of operation. Do you want a smaller nose, to lose some kilos or have a hair transplant? Is an operation the best thing for you? It might be, it might not. Visit our doctors and they'll give you the best possible advice. And your first appointment is free. All New Age Cosmetic Hospital operations are safe and our prices extremely low. Call us today. You won't regret it!

C

A: So, you want to look younger?

B: Oh yes!

A: Then forget the creams and the diets.

B: Really?

A: Exercise is the answer! Join the Power Leisure Centre and for only 60 dollars a month you'll have the choice of over 20 different sports and activities.

B: 20?!

A: Exercise regularly and in just a few weeks you'll see a change in your body.

B: I will?

A: Will you have more muscle? Yes! Will you lose fat? Yes!. Will you look healthier? Definitely! Interested?

B: I am!

A: Then fill in our application form today and we promise we'll really help you look and feel like a new person! What are you waiting for?

4.7 4C Exercise 1

Sue: Have you seen this questionnaire_in *Hi* magazine?

Deb: Not yet. What does_it say?

Sue: Well, there_are some sayings_about friendship, like, old friends_are the best friends.

Deb: Well, that's not true, I only met you last year!

Sue: Yeah. And then, it's better to have_a few really good friends than_a lot_of quite good ones.

Deb: I agree with that one.

Sue: What_about you can't buy friendship?

Deb: A lot_of people try but no, of course you can't. Next_one.

Sue: A real friend_is somebody who will lie for you.

Deb: Oh yes, that's so important. I lie for you all the time!

Sue: You do not!

Deb: All right! Only joking.

Sue: And the last_one, this_is difficult. Friendship_is stronger than love.

Deb: Oh! That_is tricky. What do you think?

4.9 4C Exercise 9

Interviewer: Hello there! Can I ask you a couple of questions?

Patrick: Sure, what about?

Interviewer: I'm doing a survey on friendship. You know, what makes a real friend?

Patrick: That's easy. For me, a real friend is somebody who will lie for you if necessary.

Interviewer: You mean, like, lie to your parents or girlfriend.

Patrick: Yeah, that's right. Also if you don't have any money, a real friend will lend you anything you need.

Interviewer: Uh-huh.

Patrick: And not keep asking for it back!

Interviewer: Thank you, that's …

Patrick: And if you tell your friend a secret, he or she won't tell anybody else.

Interviewer: That's a good …

Patrick: And another thing, if you have a problem a real friend will be there for you and help you

Interviewer: Right, I think …

Patrick: No, I haven't finished. I'm enjoying this, thanks!

Interviewer: But I …

Patrick: And, if you're looking really bad, like after a very late night, or if you're wearing clothes that don't look good at all, a real friend will tell you.

Interviewer: Yes …

Patrick: And a really good friend is a good listener. He won't interrupt you, he'll just listen. Yeah, those things make a real friend! Can I go now?

4.10 4D Exercise 3

Interviewer: Well, Andy. I don't think I've heard that before. 'I earn too much!' It's usually 'I don't earn enough!'

Andy: You see Nicole, I really wanted people to listen.

Interviewer: So, why did you say it?

Andy: It's the 21st century and I think salaries are still really unfair.

Interviewer: Well, me too! My salary's unfair. I should get much more!

Andy: Really? Anyway, look. A friend of mine works for the same company as me. We work in different offices but we have the same position. We do the same work. We do the same hours. But I earn much more than my friend. That's not fair. And what's more, I'm going to get a promotion and my friend isn't.

4.11 4D Exercise 4

Interviewer: But there must be a reason why your friend earns much less than you. Are you a better worker perhaps?

Andy: No way! She's a much quicker worker than me. She's also a lot more organised. I'm a bit faster than her on the computer, but that's all.

Interviewer: Are you more experienced or more qualified? Do you have the same qualifications?

Andy: Exactly the same. And we've both worked for the company for the same time – ten years.

Interviewer: So, why do you think you earn more?

Andy: We all know why. She's a woman!

Interviewer: And do you think this will change in the future?

Andy: I certainly hope so.

4.14 4E Exercise 7

Did you use to like the TV series *Friends*?

No, I never use to watch it.

So, what did you use to watch when you were young?

I didn't use to watch much TV at all.

4.17 4F Exercise 7

1

My mum has loads_of photo albums_of when I was young. It's great to look back through them. The bad photos really make us laugh!

2

A friend_of mine sends postcards to herself every time she goes_away! It's like a hobby I suppose but_it's_a brilliant record of what she did and how she felt. Plus you have_a picture_of all the different places.

3

I like videoing special moments. It's better than photos because you can hear people talking_ and remember how they move too. They're great to look_at when you want_a laugh!

4

I don't_understand why people write blogs. OK, if you've got something interesting to say but_a lot_of blogs_are just_about what people do every day_and_it's totally boring for_anybody_ else.

5

I still keep_a diary. I started when_I was fifteen_ and now_I am thirty-two. Every night I write_in_it just before_I go to bed. It's great fun to look back at things_I wrote when I was younger. I think you learn a lot about yourself.

4.18 Revision 4 Exercise 5

Sara: Hi Al, how are you doing?

Al: Good thanks, Sara. You?

Sara: I'm fine. Hey, I got an e-mail from your brother yesterday. He said he's having a great time in Poland.

Al: He absolutely loves it. He's been there six months on this university exchange and he wants to stay there.

Sara: Is that possible?

Al: Well, he'll ask his university here in Britain and he thinks they might say yes, but it's unusual. Most people only stay for six months and then go back to their own country.

Sara: It's difficult, isn't it?

Al: Yeah. And the other problem is accommodation. At the moment, he rents a room from the university in Warsaw. But he won't be able to stay there. He'll have to leave in four or five weeks, and then he'll need to find somewhere new to live.

Sara: Is it easy to find a flat there?

Al: He's got lots of Polish friends, so he says it won't be hard to find a new place.

Sara: Have you visited him yet?

Al: No, because I've had lots of exams on my course. They're over now, at last.

Sara: Great. What will you do when the course ends?

Al: Well, my brother has invited me to Poland, so I might go and visit him soon.

Sara: Sounds good.

(4.19) Revision 4 Exercise 8

Clare: Here you go, Beppe. A coffee and a croissant.

Beppe: Thanks Clare. Let me get this.

Clare: I've already paid. Don't worry about it.

Beppe: Well, I'll pay next week, then, OK?

Clare: Sure. You know, it's been great. I really enjoy our language exchange. I don't get many opportunities to speak Italian.

Beppe: Neither do I. I don't know any other Italians here. And I really need to improve my English.

Clare: Well, I think your English is a lot better than my Italian.

Beppe: No, not at all. Your Italian is great!

Clare: But my pronunciation is terrible.

Beppe: That's not true. I like your accent. It's sexy!

Clare: Well, so how's your job going? Are you enjoying it?

Beppe: Yes, but it's a lot harder than my last one.

Clare: Why's that?

Beppe: In my last job, I was just talking on the phone. You know, technical stuff, dealing with people's computer problems on the phone. People get very angry when their computers don't work, and it wasn't very nice.

Clare: I can imagine.

Beppe: But now, I'm programming. I'm actually writing computer programs. I earn much more money too, although I am working all the time.

Clare: Really? Well, that's great! These days, you're lucky to have a job. Lots of my friends are looking for work at the moment.

Beppe: Yeah, that's very true.

Clare: So, what kind of programming are you doing?

Beppe: Ah, OK. I'm designing a program for a bank.

Clare: Oh!

Beppe: I know. Not very exciting, but at least my workmates are a lot nicer than at my last job.

Clare: That's so important. So, you're making some Scottish friends?

Beppe: Yeah, we go out together after work on Fridays. It's great.

Clare: Nice! So, Beppe, shall we speak a bit of Italian now?

Beppe: Si! Va bene.

Activity book

(1.1) 1A Exercise 2

Georges: What do you want to do today, Carmen?

Carmen: I'm not sure. What's the weather like?

Georges: It's nice. Really sunny.

Carmen: Well, why don't we go to Sitges?

Georges: Sitges? I don't know. What's it like?

Carmen: It's cool! It's a town by the sea with lots of bars and places to go out.

Georges: Great. Can we go shopping there too?

Carmen: Yeah! Of course.

Georges: But what are the shops like?

Carmen: They're really good. Lots of nice clothes shops and some great shoe shops!

Georges: OK! Let's go! Do you want to drive?

(1.2) 1B Exercise 5

Pete: Hello?

Rick: Hi Pete, where are you?

Pete: Hi Rick. I'm on the train. We are coming to meet you now.

Rick: The train? But you usually fly here.

Pete: I know, but this is a new idea. We're travelling by train because we want to be more environmentally friendly.

Rick: Good idea. But how long does it take to get here?

Pete: It's about five hours from London to Glasgow.

Rick: Is the train nice?

Pete: Yeah, it is. We have really nice seats and there's a little café too. We're eating some sandwiches there now, and I'm reading the newspaper. Actually, you know, I prefer the train to flying.

Rick: Really? Is it more expensive?

Pete: No, the train costs the same as a plane.

Rick: Right.

Pete: Hey, what's the weather like in Glasgow?

Rick: Sorry, Pete, it's raining but maybe it'll be nice when you arrive.

Pete: Let's hope so!

(2.1) 2A Exercise 2

Woman: I love both the *Godfather* films. *The Godfather Part II* was more successful than *The Godfather* because it won six Oscars (the first film only won three!) but I prefer the original film. I think the first film is better than the sequel because Marlon Brando is in it, and he isn't in *The Godfather Part II*. One other problem is that *The Godfather Part II* is more difficult to understand than the original film. The story is really complicated. But the first film is more violent than Part II lots of people die and there is the famous scene with the horse's head in the bed! My boyfriend doesn't like that part of the film!

Man: I went to see *Raiders of the Lost Ark* with my dad when I was very little. I'm almost thirty years older now but I still love the Indiana Jones films. I don't usually like action films because I prefer more romantic films like *Sleepless in Seattle* or *Romeo and Juliet*. But the Indiana Jones films are great because they are funnier than most action films. There are quite a few jokes and they're not so serious. Actually, I thought *Indiana Jones and the Kingdom of the Crystal Skull* was more exciting than *Raiders of the Lost Ark*, maybe because it's new. I've got the original film on DVD and I watch it a lot!

1 Essential Grammar

Word order in questions → 1A

	Q	be	S	
⊕	What	's		the weather like?
⊖	Why	weren't	you	at school?
⊕		Am	I	next? Yes, you are.
⊖		Aren't	they	from Poland? No, they're Russian.

	Q	A	S	I
	What	did	you	do yesterday?
	Why	didn't	Kaka	play last week?
		Does	Lena	**enjoy** the classes? Yes, she does.
		Don't	the girls	**know** the answer? No, they don't.

1 Write T (true) or F (false).

1 In questions with the verb *be*:

  a don't use an auxiliary verb. _____

  b *be* goes after the subject. _____

  c add *not* after *be* for negatives. _____

2 In other questions:

  a the subject goes between the auxiliary and the main verb. _____

  b use the auxiliary verb *do*. _____

  c add *not* before the verb *do* for negatives. _____

be like → 1A

2 Match the questions and answers. Which two questions use *like* as a verb?

1 What are the houses like? ☐

2 What do your kids like? ☐

3 What's your teacher like? ☐

4 What would you like to drink? ☐

a Going to the beach.

b A glass of fresh orange juice.

c Quite big with a sea view.

d Really good. Lots of fun.

> **Rules**
>
> Use 'What (*be*) like?' to ask for a description.

Present simple and Present continuous → 1B

		Present continuous		
⊕	I	'm	meeting	him today.
⊖	We	aren't	doing	our homework.
❓	Is	she	arriving	now?

3 Cross out the wrong option.

1 Use *be* / *do* + *-ing* for the Present continuous.

2 Use Present *simple* / *continuous* for actions happening now.

3 Non-action verbs not usually used in the continuous form include *know, understand* and *work* / *hear*.

The future → 1B, 1C

verb form	use	
will ('ll) / won't	A Spontaneous decision B Prediction	I'll help you to carry your books. It won't rain tomorrow
may / might	C Future possibility D Decision not yet made	It **might be** cold next week. Luca **may come** for dinner tomorrow.
going to /ˈɡʌnə/	E Future plan	We're **going to stay** at the Hilton on 2 May.
Present continuous	F Future arrangement	I'm **meeting** Mark's parents tomorrow at 5 p.m.

4 Write T (true) or F (false).

1 *May* and *might* describe things which are not certain. ____

2 If you make a decision at the moment of speaking, use *going to*. ____

3 Use the Present continuous for both the present and the future. ____

4 The negative of *will* is *won't*. ____

5 Match the underlined verbs to their use, A–F.

1 Oh no! It's raining. <u>I'll get</u> the umbrella. ☐

2 <u>We're having</u> the party on Friday night. ☐

3 Lisa said <u>the weather will be</u> nice when we get to London. ☐

4 <u>I'm going to see</u> a dentist about my tooth. ☐

5 You <u>might need</u> some help tomorrow. ☐

6 Sam <u>may go</u> on holiday next month. ☐

Past continuous → 1D

➕	It	**was**	**raining.**	
➖	I	**wasn't**	**waiting**	for the bus.
❓	**Were**	you	**working**	in the library?	Yes, we were. No, we weren't.

7 Put the verbs in the Past simple or continuous.

1 We asked our teacher but she _____ the answer. (*not know*)

2 I saw Ewa on TV while she _____ the marathon. (*run*)

6 Cross out the wrong option.

1 Form the Past continuous with *was* or *were* + *-ed / -ing*.

2 Use it for an action that was *completed / in progress* at a specific time.

3 For completed past actions, use the Past *simple / continuous*.

3 It _____ when the plane landed in Moscow. (*snow*)

4 The club was closed so they _____ home. (*go*)

---

should / shouldn't → 1E

➕	I	**should**	**go**	to the dentist's.	
➖	You	**shouldn't**	**speak**	to him like that.	
❓	**Should**	we	**give**	you the homework tomorrow?	Yes, you should. No, you shouldn't.

8 Write T (true) or F (false).

1 *Should* is a modal verb, like *can* or *must*. ____

2 *Should* is followed by *-ing* or *to*. ____

3 Use *should* to give or ask for advice. ____

Articles → 1F

9 Complete with *a*, *the* or 0 (= no article) when articles are used.

> **Rules**
>
> **1** ___*a*___ talk about something for the first time
>
> **2** _____ everybody knows which thing
>
> **3** _____ a plural noun in a general way, e.g. *I love apples*
>
> **4** _____ there's only one in the world, for example, _____ US president
>
> **5** _____ with most names

10 Correct two mistakes in each sentence.

1 There's ⋏ cat in the garden. I ~~love~~ the cats! (*a*)

2 I'm not good at the languages but I do speak the Japanese.

3 Rio isn't capital city of Brazil. It's the Brasilia.

4 Xavier cut the finger and he had to see doctor.

Comparisons → 2A, 2D

	comparative	superlative	
A One syllable adjectives	+ -er	the + -est	cold → colder → the coldest
B One-syllable adjectives ending in a vowel and a consonant	double the final consonant + -er	the + double the final consonant + -est	hot → hotter → the hottest
C Most adjectives with two or more syllables.	more + adjective	the + most + adjective	gorgeous → more gorgeous → the most gorgeous
D Adjectives ending in –y	+ -ier for two-syllable adjectives	the + -iest for two syllable adjectives	easy → easier → the easiest
E Irregular	good → better → the best bad → worse → the worst		

1 Write the comparative and superlative of these adjectives, then match them to rules A–E.

bad	worse	worst	E
busy	_____	_____	☐
expensive	_____	_____	☐
fat	_____	_____	☐
young	_____	_____	☐

2 Complete with the comparative or superlative adjectives.

1 Learning Chinese is _____ than learning English. (*hard*)

2 That was _____ film I've ever seen. (*funny*)

3 Models are usually much _____ than normal people. (*thin*)

4 My dad thinks my mum is _____ woman in the world. (*beautiful*)

5 Our new car is _____ than the old one. It never works. (*bad*)

Present perfect → 2B, 2E, 3B

➕	Karl	's (has)	been	to Greece five times.
➖	They They	haven't ever 've never	studied	English before.
❓	Have	you (ever)	tried	Thai food? Yes, we have. No, we haven't.

3 Write T (true) or F (false).

1 Form the Present perfect with *have* + past participle. _____

2 The Present perfect of *have* is *have had* or *has had*. _____

3 Use the Present perfect

  a for a past action with the exact date or time, e.g. *in 2008, yesterday* _____

  b to talk about a special experience, e.g. *This is the best film I've ever seen.* _____

  c to join the past and the present, e.g. *I've lived here for six years.* _____

  d with *for* (period of time) + *since* (exact time) _____

4 Complete the sentences. Use contractions.

1 Jan _____ just sent me an email.

2 I _____ never eaten sushi before. It's delicious!

3 Ian _____ to the bank an hour ago.

4 Your mum is the most interesting person we _____ ever met.

5 _____ your sister been to Turkey?

6 It _____ rained for three months. It's too dry.

too and *enough* → 2C

Karim	is	**old**	**enough**	to take his driving test.
Your tests results	aren't	**good**	**enough**	to go to this university.
The curry	is	**too**	**hot.**	I can't eat it.

5 Complete with *too* or *enough*.

> **Rules**
>
> 1 _____ + adjective = more than necessary
>
> 2 *be* + adjective + _____ = the correct amount
>
> 3 *be* + *not* + _____ = we need more of this

6 Complete using *too* or *enough*.

1 The bag's _____ heavy. She's not strong _____ to carry it.

2 We're _____ late to catch the train! We weren't quick _____!

3 It's not big _____. It's _____ small!

so / such ... that → 2F

It was	**such**	**a**	**boring** film	(that)	I fell asleep.
The dinner was	**so**	**expensive**		(that)	we had to pay by credit card.

7 Complete with these words.

> a   cause   so   such a   that

> **Rules**
>
> 1 Use *so* and *such* to talk about the _____ of an action or situation.
>
> 2 Use _____ with an adjective + noun.
>
> 3 Use _____ with an adjective.
>
> 4 We often omit _____, especially when we speak.

8 Complete with *so*, *such* or *such a*.

1 It was _____ good party that we didn't leave until 3 a.m.!

2 It was _____ hot that it was impossible to sleep.

3 I really enjoyed meeting your parents. They're _____ nice people.

3 Essential Grammar

must / have to, mustn't / don't have to → 3A

verb form	use		
+ *must* **−** *mustn't*	explain rules and obligations (from speaker)	I **must** go to the dentist's. My tooth hurts. You **mustn't send** personal emails at work.	**Note:** You can't use *must* in the past. *I had to go to the dentist's.* (not *musted*)
+ *have to* **?**	explain rules and obligations (not from speaker)	I have to go to the dentist's. I have an appointment. **Do** I **have to pass** the test?	
− *don't have to*	Say there's a choice	You don't have to eat here if you don't want to.	

1 Write T (true) or F (false).

  1 The past of *have to* and *must* is *had to*. ____

  2 Add an *-s* to *must* with *he / she / it*. ____

  3 *Must* means the idea comes from you (the speaker!). ____

2 Write sentences. Each / = one missing word.

  1 What time / he / / start work?

  2 It's my dad's birthday so I / remember / buy him / present.

  3 We don't / / go / / party if you're tired.

  4 You / / take any photos in / airport – it's illegal.

Present perfect to join the past and the present → 3B

See *Present Perfect* on page 114.

How long	**have you been** a student?	**Since** 2001 / I was 12.
	has she had blond hair?	**For** a long time / over 10 years.

3 Complete the rules with *now, past, period, point* and *things*.

Rules

1 Use the Present perfect to talk about _____ which started in the past and are still true _____.

2 Use *How long* to ask about duration, from the _____ to now.

3 Use *for* + a _____ of time (seconds, days, months).

4 Use *since* + an exact _____ in time (a time, day or date).

---

anybody / everybody / nobody / somebody → 3C

	+	**?** / **−**	**−** meaning, **+** verb
people	1 **Somebody** called you.	Didn't **anybody** answer?	No, **nobody** could open your mobile.
things	2 I thought I saw **somebody** move.	But it wasn't **anybody**.	No, sorry. It was **nobody**.
places	3 Let's eat **somewhere**.	**Anywhere** special?	**Nowhere** expensive, please!

Rules

1 Use pronouns with *some-* when you don't say exactly who, where or what.

2 Use pronouns with *any-* in questions or with a negative verb.

3 Use pronouns with *no-* with a + verb to mean 'not one'.

4 Use pronouns with *every-* to mean 'all' the people / places / things.

4 Complete the pronouns.

  1 Is there ___where with Wi-Fi access? I'm looking for a cafe or ___where like that.

  2 ___body knows where Dan is. He didn't tell ___body where he was going.

  3 I'm going to tell you ___thing secret, so don't tell it to ___body else!

  4 ___where you go in this city, there's always ___body trying to sell you flowers.

  5 We stayed in a house in the middle of ___where. There wasn't ___thing to do.

who / which / that → 3C

A brochure is a magazine	**which / that**	**describes** holiday destinations.
A programmer is somebody	**who / that**	**writes** computer programs.
This is the game	**which / that**	**I bought** last week.

5 Cross out the wrong option.

> **Rules**
>
> 1 Use **who, where, which** or **that** + to define a *verb / noun*.
> 2 Use *who / what / that* to define a person.
> 3 Use **where** or **that** to define a *place / an event*.
> 4 Use *who / which / that* to describe a thing.

as ... as → 3D

| London | **is almost** | **as** | **expensive** | **as** | Paris. | | There | **aren't** | **as** | **many tourists** | **as** | last year. |

6 Complete using *(not) as ... as* and the adjective.

1 Judy is _____ (old) as Albert.

2 The Casio is _____ (expensive) as the Rolex.

3 Rome is _____ (hot) as Cairo today.

Subject questions → 3E

Who	**directed**	the film?
What animals	**live**	in the Amazon?
Which actor	**won**	the Oscar last year?
How many people	**went**	to the party?

7 Complete the rules with *different, subject, verb,* and *what.*

> **Rules**
>
> 1 In subject questions, the question word is the _____.
> 2 The word order is *question word* + _____.
> 3 The word order is _____ to other questions.
> 4 Form subject questions with *who, which, how many,* or _____.

Phrasal verbs → 3F, 4F

Separable phrasal verbs	I'm **filling in** the form. I'm **filling** it **in**.
Inseparable phrasal verbs	We're **looking after** my neighbour's cat.
Phrasal verbs with no object	Please **sit down**.

8 Add one word to each sentence.

> down   off   up

1 I always write new English phrases.

2 What time are we going to set tomorrow?

3 I grew in Indonesia.

4 Essential Grammar

-ing form → 4A

Subject of a sentence	Sk**ii**ng is great! Smok**ing** can kill you.
After a preposition	I'm interested **in** study**ing** French. Jaime's great **at** cook**ing**.
After some verbs, *e.g. verbs of emotion (like, love, hate)*	Lula really **enjoys making** cakes. I don't mind work**ing** late tonight.

Other verbs are followed by *to, e.g. need, want, hope, plan, promise, forget*
We decided **to speak** *to the doctor. I offered* **to wash** *my parent's car.*

1 Read the rules. Cross out the wrong form.

1 *To run / Running* is excellent exercise.

2 I hope *to see / seeing* you again soon.

3 He promised *calling / to call* me when he arrives in Bangkok.

4 Lara doesn't mind *getting up / to get up* early.

will and *might* → 4B

I	will won't	be	at home tomorrow.
You	might might not	finish	your homework tonight.

2 Complete with *might* or *will*.

1 Use _____ to make predictions when you're quite sure.

2 Use _____ to make predictions when you aren't very sure.

3 Use *may* in the same way as _____ .

first conditional → 4C

If	I	**see**	Bob,	I	**'ll (will)**	**tell**	him your news.
If	we	**don't leave**	now,	we	**won't**	**catch**	the bus.

3 Circle the correct rule.

> **Rules**
>
> 1 Use the First conditional to talk about a *possible / impossible* future situation.
>
> 2 Form the First conditional with **if** + *Present simple / will*, and **will** + verb.
>
> 3 Use a comma (,) when the *if*-clause comes *at the beginning / in the middle of* the sentence.

4 Complete with these verbs.

1 If you _____ your exams, your grandma _____ you a new bike.   (pass, buy)

2 We _____ the game if Frank _____ in the team.   (not win, not be)

3 If they _____ me their e-mail address, I _____ them the photos.   (give, send)

much, a lot, a little, a bit + comparative → 4D

Pekka is	**much**	quicker	than	Timo.
The hotel is	**a lot**	more expensive	than	the youth hostel.
Sachin is	**a little**	more organised	than	the other students.
The buses are	**a bit**	slower	than	the trains.

5 Write the missing words.

1 Irena _____ _____ lot happier in her new job.

2 That mobile phone is €500! It's _____ _____ expensive than the others!

3 Viktor took some medicine yesterday so he _____ _____ little better today.

4 People from Europe are a _____ more passionate _____ people from my country.

used to → 4E

My dad	**used to**	live	in Bulgaria.
She	**didn't used to**	like	sports.
Did	you	**use to**	work	here?

Then

Now

6 Cross out the wrong option.

1 **Used to** describes something in the past which *doesn't happen / still happens* today.

2 **Used to** is the *same / different* for all persons.

3 The question form of **used to** is Did you *used to / use to* … ?

7 Look at Rob then and now. Complete with *used to / didn't use to* and the verbs.

1 Rob _____ glasses. (*wear*)

2 He _____ the guitar. (*play*)

3 He _____ his bedroom. (*tidy*)

4 He _____ wearing hats. (*like*)

Verb + *back* → 4F
See Phrasal verbs on page 117.

I'll have to go **back** because I forgot my umbrella.
After his divorce, Si moved **back** to his mum's flat.

Back means *again* or *in the opposite direction.*

8 Complete with *back* + the verbs.

| call | come | get | give | take |

1 That's my pen. Please _____ it _____ to me.

2 Sorry, we're closed. Please _____ _____ tomorrow.

3 **A:** Sue's not here. Do you want to leave a message?
B: Don't worry, I'll _____ _____ later.

4 The film was so long we didn't _____ _____ home until midnight.

5 My phone doesn't work, so I'm _____ it _____ to the shop.

Richmond Publishing
58 St. Aldates
Oxford
OX1 1ST
United Kingdom

© Santillana Educación S.L. / Richmond Publishing, 2010

ISBN: 978-84-668-0701-2

Printed by Orymu, S.A.
D.L. M-1480-2010

Project Development: Rhona Snelling, Sarah Thorpe
Editor: May Corfield, Rhona Snelling
Design and Layout: Nigel Jordan, Lorna Heaslip
Cover Design: Aqueduct, London and Richmond Publishing
Photo Research: Magdalena Mayo
Audio Production: Ian Harker

Richmond Essential English Course is an adaptation of *Interlink* (© Learning Factory, Ltda.)
Published under licence by Learning Factory Ltda.

The publishers would like to thank the original *Interlink* writing team:
Ricardo Sili, Paula Boyce, Carla Chaves, Virginia Garcia, Sueli Büsmayer, Angela Dias

My sincere thanks to Carmen Dolz for all her consistently wise feedback, creative suggestions and ideas, together with her patient, selfless support. A large thank you is due too to Camila de Abreu e Souza, for all her excellent reflective and imaginative input. I'd like to thank Lula and Calum for their constant inspiration and the countless hours they've given to the project too. I'd also like to thank Rhona for all her hard work and all the anonymous teachers whose work has inspired REEC. You know who you are!
(Paul Seligson)

Every effort has been made to trace the holders of copyright before publication. The publishers will be pleased to rectify any error or omission at the earliest opportunity.

Illustrations:
David Banks, Phil Hackett, Ben Hasler, Matt Latchford, Ben Swift, Graham White

Photographs:
J. Jaime; Krauel; S. Enríquez; A. G. E. FOTOSTOCK; ACI AGENCIA DE FOTOGRAFÍA/Alamy Images, Peter Mountain; ALBUM; COMSTOCK; CORDON PRESS; COVER/CORBIS; EFE/PANA JIJI/*Takahashi;* FOTONONSTOP; GETTY IMAGES SALES SPAIN/Bill Losh, David Goddard, Mike Marsland, Thomas Kokta, Caroline von Tuempling, Wirelmage/Jesse Grant, Gene Kornman, Ebet Roberts, Time & Life Pictures, A. Chederros, Mark Harris, George Doyle, Paul Conrath, AFP, AFP/Kazuhiro Nogi, Keren Su, Peter Dazeley, Stephen Frink, Thomas Schweizer, Anna Watson, Peter Cade, Crowther&Carter, Camille Moirenc, Matt Cardy, Sergio Pitamitz, Tim Mosenfelder, Munawar Hosain, Hulton Archive, Tanya Constantine, William B. Plowman, Phil Dent, Tom Stoddart Archive, AFP/Bertrand Langlois, Michael Ochs Archives, Digital Vision, David Levenson, Jerry Marks Productions, Ghislain & Marie David de Lossy, Nancy Ney; HIGHRES PRESS STOCK/AbleStock.com; ISTOCKPHOTO; MELBA AGENCY; PHOTODISC; Joe Kolman; BFI; SERIDEC PHOTOIMAGENES CD/ DigitalVision; ©A.M.P.A.S; ARCHIVO SANTILLANA